THE
Sommelier's
Cookbook

THE
Sommelier's Cookbook

Recipes and Wine Pairings for Discerning Palates

JOANIE MÉTIVIER

Photography by Andrew Purcell

**ROCKRIDGE
PRESS**

For general information on our other products and services or to obtain technical support, please contact our Customer Care Department within the United States at (866) 744-2665, or outside the United States at (510) 253-0500.

Rockridge Press publishes its books in a variety of electronic and print formats. Some content that appears in print may not be available in electronic books, and vice versa.

TRADEMARKS: Rockridge Press and the Rockridge Press logo are trademarks or registered trademarks of Callisto Media Inc. and/or its affiliates, in the United States and other countries, and may not be used without written permission. All other trademarks are the property of their respective owners. Rockridge Press is not associated with any product or vendor mentioned in this book.

Interior and Cover Designer: Lisa Forde
Art Producer: Meg Baggott
Editor: Cecily McAndrews
Production Editor: Jenna Dutton

Photography © 2020 Andrew Purcell
Food styling by Carrie Purcell

Cover: Beet Carpaccio & Goat Cheese with Pink Grapefruit Dressing

ISBN: Print 978-1-64739-809-5
       eBook 978-1-64739-484-4
R0

*To all the passionate individuals
I've had the chance to share a glass of
wine with, and to all the future ones.*

Chilled Zucchini
Noodles with
Coconut-Peanut
Sauce (page 181):
PAIR WITH:
Aromatic Whites
page 57

Contents

Introduction viii

PART I: THE WINE

PART II: THE FOOD

Introduction

When you ask people why they love wine, their answers tend to be quite romantic: It's the people behind the scene; it's the act of sharing; it's an infinite source of discoveries rich in history, culture, and passion. This is all true and beautifully put; I'm always the first to praise the intricate and complex world of wine in all its glory. However, in reality, it all comes down to taste. We drink wine because we like it.

As a sommelier and a wine journalist, I've had the chance to travel the world, try wines in the most spectacular settings, discover traditional and cultural practices firsthand, and dine in fabulous high-end restaurants as well as the coolest local joints. However, my most memorable experiences are not necessarily the most luxurious ones, but rather the moments when everything seems to fall into place, when time seems to slow down, and the food, wine, and company just make you happy. Wine pairings don't have to be fancy. Just think of how a good burger can make you feel. Now, imagine having a glass of wine that enhances the juiciness of the meat or transforms the crispiness of your fries into something ethereal. That's an exciting pairing!

Eating like a sommelier doesn't necessarily mean following every rule in this book. It simply means that you'll be equally excited by the delicious dish you've cooked and by the thought of opening that cool bottle you've been dying to try. You can always play around with a recipe and adapt it. But if you do that with a specific wine to pair it with in mind, it gives the whole process a purpose. Or, try it the other way around: Use the food to narrow down your selection and, if you're lucky, discover a whole new world of wine. Eating like a sommelier also means getting excited about trying out new flavors combinations or experimenting with pairings. It starts with a passion for learning, a strong interest in gastronomy and viticulture, and infinite curiosity.

How to Use This Book

This book is divided into two sections: One is all about wine and the other is all about food. These complementary partners each play a unique role that deserves to be understood separately and together. Start by choosing a bottle or a dish, then fall down the rabbit hole to a better understanding of good food and wine. Feel free to read out of order—refer to the appendices for Six Perfect Party Pairings (page 221), take in the Take-Out Pairings (page 227), or skim the useful glossary of wine terms (page 229). Just follow your nose to whatever appeals to you. It will lead somewhere delicious.

The Wine

This section will help you gain the knowledge and confidence to find exactly what you need and want when wine shopping. It will help you understand the basics and fundamentals of wine pairing; how flavors, texture, and structure work together; and which styles of wines are better suited to food than others. The following chapters will be separated by style: sparkling and sweet wines, followed by white and red wines. I want you to understand the character of popular grape varieties that you already know as well as discover new varieties that you may enjoy. To that end, wine profiles have been organized from lighter to heavier so that you may browse the selection with logic and ease. The complex world of wine can be overwhelming at first, but this book will be your guide to educate your palate and understand your very own taste.

The Food

The second section of this book is devoted exclusively to recipes. I've created 75 different dishes, from simple snacks to mains and desserts, all designed specifically to pair with wine. These recipes are simple, varied, and flavorful, from bar snack favorites like Chicken Wings with Spicy Maple Barbecue Sauce (page 118) and Barbecue Spareribs (page 210), to new classics such as Ahi Tuna Tacos with Aioli (page 198) and Hoisin Chicken Lettuce Wraps (page 164), and plant-based eats like Roasted Vegetable Chili with Crème Fraîche (page 188) and Sweet Potatoes Stuffed with Brussels Sprouts, Cranberries & Cashews (page 190). Some are recipes you'll want to make for a weeknight dinner and others are recipes for a special occasion. Either way, these recipes will make you want to open a bottle of wine. Once you taste the way a successful pairing can elevate both the food and the wine, it will open your eyes to a whole different way of eating and drinking. You'll find that not only is it easy to choose your own complementary pairings, it's also fun.

PART I

THE WINE

A good pairing is a subtle and delicate interaction. You shouldn't expect fireworks, but rather a sense of harmony, like the food and the wine are shaking hands in agreement. Let's explore what you need to take into consideration, on your plate and in the glass, to create a good match.

Chapter 1

Wine & Food: A Love Story

Wine and food are in a committed relationship—a relationship based on trust and respect. For a pairing to work out, the wine must bond with the food. This connection can be achieved in numerous ways: through unity or contrast, aromas or texture, intensity or style. However, if anything troubles this sense of harmony, like an overpowering ingredient or bitter tannins, the love story may fall apart completely. It's a delicate affair, but not a complicated one. After learning a few basics, you'll be able to eat and drink with confidence and even have fun experimenting. We will get to specific wines in good time, but for now, familiarize yourself with these principles.

A Few Basic Principles of Wine Pairing

Wine pairing, and taste in general, are very subjective: What tastes good to you might not appeal to everyone. However, there are a few basic rules that apply to pairings and these are quite universal.

Intensity and texture. The intensity or complexity of the bottle or the dish you want to pair must be equal or similar: simple with simple, bold with bold. The same goes for texture, or mouthfeel: a smooth, creamy sauce or strong tannins in a wine translate to sensations that can impact your taste. Nothing should be overpowering. If it's a match, everyone's a winner.

When in doubt, add bubbles. Sparkling wines are one of the most versatile in terms of pairing. When you don't have any other options, it's a safe go-to.

Versatile wines are now your best friends. High-acidity, medium-bodied wines such as Riesling or Grüner Veltliner (Crisp & Edgy Whites, page 43, or Aromatic Whites, page 57) can work with a broad range of foods. They're cleansing for your palate and can adapt to all sorts of flavors, from Chinese takeout to a tarte flambée.

"Red with meat, white with fish" is not true. You may have heard this rule repeatedly when it comes to food and wine pairing. With the vast array of fish and meat, not to mention wines, do you really think such a broad generalization holds up? Some lighter style of fruity reds (Delicate Reds, page 74) may even be better suited to your pescatarian plate.

Local food with local wines. A fun way to explore pairings is with local culture in mind. What grows together, goes together—as the saying goes—and it couldn't be truer. Think about great, classic pairings like boeuf Bourguignon and Pinot Noir or Barolo and white truffles. There are countless examples. However, it's important to stay open-minded. Regional cuisines can be seen as a starting point for your pairing inspiration, but should not limit you in any way. In some cases, local delicacies just don't make sense. Have you ever tried Port and sardines? It's a match made in hell!

Things to Consider When Pairing Wine with Food

When contemplating a glass of wine, there are many factors to consider. Knowing the vocabulary, what to analyze, and how to go about it is part of every professional wine tasting. It's also the best way to approach a food and wine pairing at home.

Tannins

Tannins are phenolic compounds found primarily in the skins and pits of grapes. Since white wines only have limited skin contact, they rarely have tannins, but red wines, which always macerate with the skins to get their color, always have tannins. Tannins are astringent, tactile, and have a drying sensation you can feel on your palate. They are also part of what provides structure to a wine. Structure connotes all the components you can taste on your palate: fruit, acid, tannin, sugar, and alcohol. The stronger these elements are, the more structured and heavier the wine is. Tannins need fat. The proteins in the fat bond with the tannin and soften both: It's why fatty steaks melt in your mouth when paired with a tannic wine and why people add cream to tannic Earl Grey tea. But tread lightly with tannins, as they can easily ruin your pairing. For instance, one of the Powerful Reds (page 89) can destroy your palate for a delicate piece of fish. It's all about understanding what works together.

Acidity

Acidity is the crisp, lively character in a wine. This is what activates your salivary glands and makes you want another glass. Acidity is the backbone of every pairing. It can make your rich, creamy dish seem light and elegant. It can hold up against tart ingredients and is the answer to hard-to-pair ingredients like asparagus or artichokes. Acidity is the key element to make your pairing shine, and make you anticipate the next bite. However, the acidity of your wine must always be equal or superior to the acidity in the dish. An appropriate pairing will make the food and wine sing, whereas an imbalanced one will fall flat.

Alcohol Level

Alcohol is the result of **fermentation**. **Yeast** transforms the natural sugars found in grapes into alcohol. Most wines will range between 12 percent and 14 percent but can go as high as 17 percent for table wines and 22 percent for fortified wines. As it translates to flavor, high-alcohol wines will enhance spiciness. It also goes both ways: Spice in a dish may magnify the perception of alcohol in your wine. When pairing high-alcohol wines, opt for aromatic herbs and savory seasonings instead of sharp spices. High alcohol and sweet flavors are usually a good bet, too.

Sweetness

Sweetness in wines is referred to as "residual sugar." It's the leftover natural sugars after fermentation has stopped. Your wine should always be sweeter than your dish; otherwise, the wine will taste flat. Sweet dishes have a coating effect; they make your taste buds temporarily accustomed to the elevated sugar levels. This means that a dry wine will feel even more acidic than normal after a bite of something sweet, whereas a sweeter wine will feel lighter and more balanced. Not to mention, sweetness lessens spiciness. Slightly sweet wines or off-dry options (like Riesling, page 57) are ideal for a meal with a kick.

Body

Body refers to the perception of volume on the palate. You could compare it with types of milk. Skim is equivalent to light-bodied wines, whereas heavy cream is similar to full-bodied wines. The body is often an overlooked characteristic of wine pairing. We tend to think the acidity will make everything work, but it's not always the case. Matching the body of the wine and the dish can create harmony that, though sometimes rather subtle, can be very satisfying.

Aromas & Flavors

Aromas are the scents we smell in a wine, whereas flavors are the tastes we experience while sipping it. For any successful pairing, aromas are a secondary concern. Once the actual palate of the wine seems to fit (acidity, body, texture, and so on), you can push the pairing even further. Consider aromas with two options in mind. You can match the aroma compounds of the wine with ingredients in your dish, making a congruent or echoing pairing. For example, a typical aroma in Chilean Cabernet Sauvignon is mint; by using the same flavor in your dish, you'll emphasize this specific taste. On the other hand, it's also fun to make contrasting pairings, like a sweet-savory combination that pairs the caramelized aromas of aged Port with salty nuts.

Things to Consider When Pairing Food with Wine

Besides the few basic principles explained in the following section, there are no specific rules when pairing food with wine. The goal is to successfully create harmony, which can be achieved is so many ways. It's up to you to find what fits your taste.

The Components

You should consider the recipe as a whole, as well as the individual ingredients that go into it. The same piece of chicken could be paired with almost every style or color of wine, but it's the preparation method—the texture (is it crunchy fried chicken?), the sauce (barbecue?), the spices (is it a Moroccan tagine?)—that dictates what goes best with it. In some cases, a cooking method such as poaching, searing, grilling, or braising may be more important than the protein itself, as it brings different flavors, texture, and intensity to the dining experience. The same logic can apply to various styles of dishes. Just imagine trying to pair a plate of pasta with wine: Would you consider the pasta or the sauce for the pairing? The most important source of flavor (the sauce) may not always be the primary ingredient (the pasta).

Complexity

All dishes are not created equal. Some are straightforward, with just a few ingredients or cooking steps; others can be extremely involved. A dish's complexity should be reflected in your choice of wine. It's a question of balance—you don't want a complex wine that overpowers your simple dish or an easygoing wine to underwhelm a layered recipe. A perfect pairing is a complementary one.

Wine Killers

Beware of strong flavors. Don't get me wrong, bold flavors such as spice and heat can absolutely work with wine. However, there are a few foods that are tricky, even almost impossible, to pair successfully. We call them wine killers. Pickled vegetables or anything heavy on vinegar is to be avoided at all costs. The acidity in the vinegar often overpowers wines and lends a sour note. Other problematic foods include asparagus, which contains a sulfur compound that gives the wine a metallic taste, and artichokes, which ratchet up the taste of wine to a saccharine sweetness because of a compound called cynarin. It's not impossible to pair these wine killers, but it's a challenge to be sure, especially when they are part of a larger dish. The best way around this is to choose the most versatile of wines: Sparkling Wines (page 21) and Crisp & Edgy Whites (page 43).

Salt

Salt can be either a blessing or a nuisance. When paired with a fresh, crisp, high-acidity wine (like Crisp & Edgy Whites, page 43), the salt will enhance the freshness. It gives it a little boost of deliciousness, as long as the saltiness is not exaggerated. With a glass of sweet wine (see Sweet & Fortified Wines, page 31), you'll also have that sweet and savory combination that everyone loves. However, when paired with strong and bold tannins, the flavors may feel imbalanced because both tannins and salt are dehydrating components.

Umami

Umami flavors come from a molecule called glutamate, which is found in ingredients such as mushrooms, meats, and aged cheeses. This flavor can be described as savory and satisfying, and can be beautifully enhanced with the right pairing. For example, a mushroom risotto paired with a Burgundy Pinot Noir will draw out those deep flavors. **Aromatic** wines, as well as aged or oxidative wines, can heighten umami in food. **Oxidation** is the key to teasing out earthy, nutty, leathery tertiary aromas, which are fantastic with umami-laced foods.

FOOD & WINE PAIRING CHEAT SHEET

FOOD CHARACTERISTICS	IMPACT ON WINE		WINE TO MATCH
	INCREASES ⇄	DECREASES	
ACIDITY	Fruitiness Richness Sweetness	Acidity	Aromatic Whites (page 57) Crisp & Edgy Whites (page 43) Delicate Reds (page 74) Friendly, Moderate Reds (page 79)
BITTERNESS	Bitterness		Delicate Reds (page 74) Friendly, Moderate Reds (page 79)
SALT	Richness Smoothness	Acidity Astringency Bitterness	Aromatic Whites (page 57) Crisp & Edgy Whites (page 43) Sparkling Wines (page 21) Sweet Wines (Sweet & Fortified Wines, page 31)
SPICE	Alcohol		Sweet Wines (Sweet & Fortified Wines, page 31)
SWEET	Acidity Astringency Bitterness	Body Fruit Richness Sweetness	Sparkling Wines (page 21) Sweet & Fortified Wines (page 31)
UMAMI	Acidity Astringency Bitterness	Body Fruitiness Sweetness	Delicate Reds (page 74) Friendly, Moderate Reds (page 79) Powerful Reds (page 89) Rich & Bold Whites (page 62)

PAIRING WITH NATURAL WINES

Natural wines are a popular trend lately. The actual definition of natural wine has been heavily debated. Natural wines come from everywhere in the world, although most are French or Italian, and the fact that they are natural is not always indicated on the label. Some will use the monikers "nature," "natural" or "low intervention," but these are not official terms. Recognized in France only since March 2020, a new denomination will now be put in place using the term "vin méthode nature." For now, it's the only recognized and controlled designation. In short, natural wines are made from organic grapes harvested by hand and vinified with indigenous yeast, without any input or corrective oenology technique and no added sulfites. In terms of pairings, natural wines can be a wild card. I'd recommend tasting the bottle before trying to pair it, as you never know what to expect.

To learn more about orange wine and pétillant naturel, check out the information on pages 19 and 41.

Serving Like a Somm

Sommeliers understand how the environment and service can impact the taste of the wine. A few factors beyond what's in the bottle can change the taste dramatically. Keep them in mind to get the full experience a wine has to offer.

Getting the Temperature Right

Temperature is one of the most important things to get right when serving wine. If it's too cold, it won't show all of its aromatic potential. If it's too warm, the texture and alcohol will take the lead and the wine will feel heavy and unbalanced.

These are the ideal temperature ranges for the following wine categories.

- Sparkling Wines (page 21) and Sweet & Fortified Wines (page 31): 40° to 50°F

- Crisp & Edgy Whites (page 43), Aromatic Whites (page 57), and Rosé Wines (page 66): 44° to 55°F

- Rich & Bold Whites (page 62): 50° to 55°F

- Delicate Reds (page 74): 54° to 56°F

- Friendly, Moderate Reds (page 79): 56 to 60°F

- Powerful Reds (page 89): 61° to 65°F

The fastest way to chill a bottle of wine is in an ice bucket filled with half ice and half water. You can use the fridge or even the freezer, as long as you don't forget your bottle is in there. Since the bottle will warm as soon as it's out of your fridge or wine cellar, it's always better to start it off a little bit colder to eventually reach the perfect temperature.

To Decant or Not Decant?

There are two reasons why you might want to pour the content of your bottle into a nice decanter. The first is to separate clear wine from deposits in the bottom of the bottle. Deposits, or dregs, are the residue that accumulates at the bottom of the bottle when a wine ages, especially in Powerful Reds (page 89). They're harmless, but you might want to keep them out of your glass.

Another reason to use a decanter is to aerate the wine. The transfer will bring oxygen in the wine and may open up the aromas or even clear some faulty traits such as unpleasant smells (like rotten eggs or burnt matches) that may occur in some wines. These are faults that can disappear after an hour or so in a decanter. Wine is a living thing, and observing its evolution once it encounters oxygen is a fun process. I recommend tasting it when you first decant it and then an hour later to see if you detect any changes.

Serving Smarts

Glassware needs to be clean, dry, and without residual odor. In terms of sizes and shape, have some good-quality universal, standard stemmed glassware. They'll have a rounded bowl with a narrow rim and a volume of at least 10 ounces, so you have room to swirl. These are good for every style of wine—red, white, sparkling, and others.

Stemless may look cool, but you'll just end up warming your wine with your hands. An error that most people make is choosing different glasses for sparkling wines and dessert wines. If the glass is too small or narrow, you can't swirl or smell properly, and the quality of the tasting will be impaired. This is why flutes are never recommended. They might look festive, but by virtue of their narrow shape, they can't render the full aromatic profile of a wine. Always stick with standard stemmed glassware, no matter what you're drinking.

Tips for Cooking with Wine

Wine is a companion to food in many ways. It can also be an ingredient in cooking, and its unique flavors are able to give a helping hand in many dishes.

You can't fix a bad wine by cooking with it. The wine you choose to cook with will, of course, affect the final results. No one likes throwing wine out, but if the wine is bitter, sour, or just undrinkable, it won't miraculously become good if it's cooked. That's why cooking wines should never be used in a recipe: They're low quality, loaded with salt, and won't do your food any favors.

Different styles of wine will give different flavors. Take into account the sweetness, acidity, body, and tannins of the wine as well as the flavors. A bright and crisp wine will add acidity, whereas a fruity red will bring the same aromas to the plate.

Equilibrate acids. If you use a high-acidity wine when cooking, reduce the amount of other acidic ingredients such as lemon juice or vinegar. The wine will serve as a replacement.

Don't forget sweet and fortified wines. Fortified wines have very concentrated flavors that can withstand cooking and bring major flavor to a dish. Marsala, Port, Sherry, and Madeira all have unique aromatic profiles that can take your dish to a whole new level. To understand the different styles, check out the full section of Sweet & Fortified Wines (page 31).

Consider your cooking method. Reserve your lesser-quality bottles for braises, marinades, or stews, because the alcohol will have time to evaporate and the flavors will be integrated. But if you add wine at the end of a preparation, use the good stuff, as it will retain its original flavors.

Chapter 2

Sparkling, Sweet & Fortified Wines

SPARKLING WINES

SWEET & FORTIFIED WINES

Know Your Bubbly

Nothing says fun quite like a bottle of bubbly. The production of sparkling wines started sometime in the early 16th century. The exact origins remain unclear, as various producing regions have early written proof of sparkle in their bottles, but we know it all started as an accident and was, at first, considered a flaw. As this appearance of bubbles became better understood and controlled, people developed a taste for it. Sparkling wine production became popular in Champagne in the early 18th century.

Though Champagne is by far the most famous example, sparkling wines are produced all around the world. It has successfully transitioned from a drink reserved for aristocracy to a pleasure everyone can enjoy.

The most recognized technique to produce sparkling wines is the traditional method, also called "méthode champenoise." This involves provoking a second fermentation in a base wine by adding a mixture of yeast and sugar called liqueur de tirage to the bottle. The wines are then aged on the **lees** (dead yeast) from the liqueur de tirage for at least 15 months, which will provide the autolytic flavors of bread, brioche, crackers, yeast, and nuts. (**Autolysis** is a chemical reaction between the wine and the lees by which enzymes break down the dead yeast cells and add richness and a specific aromatic profile.)

The more time the wine spends on the lees, the more present those unique flavors will be. The dead yeasts and sediments are then removed with a process called **disgorgement**, and the bottle is topped up with a mixture of fresh wine and sugar called liqueur de dosage. This determines the sweetness level and style of the final product. This method makes the most elegant and finest bubbles as well as the most complex, rich, long-lived sparkling wines.

However, the second fermentation is also the most expensive and time-consuming. The **Charmat** method, also called "tank method" or "cuve close," is a quicker and more affordable way to make sparkling wine. The second fermentation happens in a pressurized tank to a large volume of wine instead of individually in each bottle. Wines produced from this method are usually youthful and easy drinking because they don't undergo an aging period. Since this method is such a rapid, efficient way to make large volumes of wine, it's always the most affordable option.

Sparkling wine can be found in so many colors and styles: white, rosé, and even red, from bone-dry to lusciously sweet. There's a perfect sparkling wine for every dish.

Decoding Sparkling Wine Labels

A bottle of sparkling wine has a lot to say. The style and level of sweetness can both be found on the label.

Vintage

The year a sparkling wine was made, known as **vintage**, is not always present on the wine label. Most sparkling wines are blends of fresh wines from the most recent vintage and reserve wines that were preserved from previous years. However, if you do see a vintage, a year indicated on the label, this means the producer thought the year was particularly unique or of high enough quality to make a vintage wine. Vintage wines often have longer aging period requirements (a minimum of three years, whereas the minimum for non-vintage Champagne is 15 months) and will have more autolytic character of brioche, yeast, marzipan, crème brûlée, or nutty aromas as well as complexity and body.

Dosage

Dosage, the last step in sparkling winemaking, involves the addition of liqueur de dosage, a mixture of fresh wine and sugar that will determine the sweetness level of the final product. Dosage is probably one of the most important pieces of information on your sparkling wine label. In Champagne, the scale goes from Extra Brut (driest) to Doux (sweetest).

BRUT NATURE OR ZÉRO DOSAGE:	0 to 3 grams per liter of residual sugar
EXTRA BRUT:	0 to 6 grams per liter of residual sugar
BRUT:	0 to 12 grams per liter of residual sugar
EXTRA DRY:	12 to 17 grams per liter of residual sugar
DRY:	17 to 32 grams per liter of residual sugar
DEMI-SEC:	32 to 50 grams per liter of residual sugar
DOUX:	50 or more grams per liter of residual sugar

Other sparkling wines in the world often use the same terms to effectively indicate the sweetness level of their wines, although the permitted level of residual sugar may vary slightly from one category to the other and the terms may be translated depending on country. For example, "Doux" may be called "Dulce" in Spain.

Blanc de Blancs & Blanc de Noirs

Blanc de Blancs Champagne or other sparkling wines indicate that only a white grape **varietal** has been used for production, which is usually Chardonnay. Blanc de blancs sparkling wines tend to be very crisp and elegant with vibrant acidity and a fresh style.

Blanc de noirs uses only red grape varietals. They'll have more structure and red fruit aromas. These terms were introduced in Champagne but are now used for sparkling wines around the globe, and even for still wines in some cases.

EVERYTHING YOU NEED TO KNOW
ABOUT PÉT-NAT

The wine world is abuzz about pét-nat wines (short for pétillant naturel). But what are they and, most important, what should you eat with them? Contrary to popular belief, these wines are not necessarily made with organic grapes, and they're not a subgroup of natural wines. A producer will often use low intervention and eco-friendly grapes, but pét-nat refers only to the method used to make the wine. Pétillant naturel ("naturally sparkling" in French) wines are made from an old method called méthode ancestrale. Simply put, the wine is bottled before the fermentation is complete. Hence, the carbon dioxide produced by the transformation of sugar into alcohol gets stuck and integrated into the bottle. It's the easiest method to create a sparkling effect, or at least one with very few steps. Pétillants naturels are not bound to a specific region, as this method of production can be done anywhere, but a few areas in France are known for their production. In 2007, Montlouis-sur-Loire in the Loire Valley regulated the term "pétillant originel" to distinguish their pét-nat production from their traditional method sparkling wines. Gaillac, just north of Toulouse, and Limoux in Languedoc are also recognized as pét-nat producers, but you'll also find many coming from Italy. The quickest way to recognize a pét-nat is to look at the closure: They use crown caps instead of corks. Some bottles may also be labeled as "méthode ancestrale" or "col fondo," which is the Italian equivalent to pét-nat. It's also worth noting that pét-nat can be found in all sorts of colors: light gold, deep orange, bright pink, or red. Since there are not many regulations, any grape varietal can be used. Zweigelt and Blaufränkisch make stunning red pét-nat, for example.

Pét-nats have a fizzy mouthfeel, are generally low in alcohol, and often **cloudy** in appearance. In most cases, they'll also have residual sugar. They can be quite versatile with food since they're lightly sparkling and fresh. Try them with cheeses, charcuterie boards, sushi, fresh vegetables, and more.

Know Your Sweet & Fortified Wines

These flavorful wines are definitely not as sought-after as they once were. They were the wines of choice of the French royal court in the 1700s, and were considered a luxury product throughout the century that followed. It's about time for a renaissance. Simply put, sweet and and fortified wines are fantastic with food. I refuse to call them dessert wines as they are in no way limited to the end of the meal. They are deliciously luscious and intense with unique flavor profiles and textures. Sweetness is your friend, especially when considering wine pairing. Think of classic duos such as Sherry with jamón ibérico, or Sauternes with foie gras.

You can get the most concentrated fruity character from young bottles of Port (page 31), intense savory and nutty flavors from Sherry (page 33), and luscious caramel and exotic notes from late harvests (page 36). Skip the small dessert glasses and use your regular glasses to be able to get all the aromatic potential.

Sweet wine production has a very specific goal. In sweet winemaking, the aim is to concentrate flavors by reducing the water content in the grapes. Winemakers use various techniques to achieve this.

First, there's fortification. Fortified wines vary in color, style, taste, sweetness (not all of them are sweet), and alcohol level, but they all have one thing in common: At some point during production, a distillate (neutral spirit) is added. This stops fermentation, which leaves some of the initial sugar intact and increases the alcohol levels.

Most other techniques concentrate the sugar content directly in the grapes either by drying the grapes (such as in Appassimento, Recioto, and Vin Santo), by letting them get to maximum maturity (i.e. late harvest), by allowing the growth of noble rot, a mold that causes grapes to shrivel when controlled (wines like Sauternes, Coteaux du Layon, and Tokaj) or by leaving the grapes to freeze (ice wines). In some cases, the addition of a sweetener is allowed, mostly before fermentation, but it's not a widespread technique.

Sparkling Wines

CHAMPAGNE

Pronunciation: sham·PEIN

Where It's Made: Exclusively in the Champagne region of France

Recommended Producers: Champagne Deutz, Champagne Billecart-Salmon, Champagne Jacques Selosse, Champagne Pol Roger, Champagne Henriot, Champagne Ruinart, Champagne de Venoge, Champagne Bollinger, Champagne Chartogne-Taillet

Overarching Characteristics: Elegant, noble, fine bubbles, brioche, orchard fruits, cream, nutty, from lean and zesty to rich and creamy

Not all sparkling wine is Champagne! The name refers only to the sparkling wines produced in the region of Champagne. The northern location, cool climate, and special chalky soils are responsible for the unique brightness and flavors of Champagne. The region is separated into 319 villages that have been classified for the quality of their **terroir**. Of these, 42 have been granted Premier **Cru** level and 17 Grand Cru, the latter being the very best vineyard sites. Äy and Bouzy Grand Cru are recognized for the quality of their black grapes and Avize, Cramant, and Le Mesnil for Chardonnay.

Champagne is made predominantly from three main grape varieties: Pinot Noir, Meunier, and Chardonnay. They're each responsible for specific characteristics in the wine. Chardonnay brings elegance, freshness, and acidity to the blends. Pinot Noir brings structure, red fruit aromas, assertiveness, and body. Meunier brings suppleness, fruitiness, and roundness.

Champagnes are made following the traditional method, also called méthode champenoise (page 16). The wines are aged in ancient limestone quarries called crayères. The deep and long chalk tunnels offer the perfect temperature and humidity control for the delicate pressurized bottles.

Good with: Literally everything! From light dishes to crispy fried things, rich sauces, and even desserts, you can't go wrong. Pair classic Brut Champagne with caviar, sushi, light fish, seafood, mac and cheese, and triple cream cheeses. Pair Extra-Dry or Brut Nature Champagne with lobster, chips, or chicken dishes. Pair rosé Champagne with duck, crab, charcuterie, or roasted pork. Pair sweet Champagne with spicy dishes, berries and fruit desserts, mascarpone, or pastries.

Try It with These Recipes: Bacon-Asiago Popcorn (page 105), Bacon-Wrapped Dates with Goat Cheese (page 107), Lemony Onion Rings (page 113), Crab Cakes with Tangerine Salsa (page 158)

Also Try: *Franciacorta, Cava, Crémant*

CRÉMANT

Pronunciation: cray·MAHN

Where It's Made: Nine regions can produce Crémant, eight of which are in France: Loire, Bordeaux, Alsace, Bourgogne, Jura, Savoie, Die, and Limoux, plus Luxembourg.

Recommended Producers: Domaine Bott-Geyl (Alsace), Langlois-Chateau (Loire), Les Cordeliers (Bordeaux), Bailly-Lapierre (Bourgogne), Domaine J. Laurens (Limoux), André et Mireille Tissot (Jura)

Overarching Characteristics: Delicate, elegant, citrus, toast, well-balanced

The word "Crémant" actually originated in the Champagne region to designate wines that were less effervescent, but the term has not been associated with Champagne since 1985. Crémant are sparkling wines made with the traditional method in specific regions, using local grapes. They are usually very good quality and more affordable than Champagne. The regulations vary depending on the region, but they all have a minimum aging of 12 months, compared to 15 months for non-vintage Champagne.

CRÉMANT D'ALSACE: Alsace produces half of the overall French Crémant production. Most Crémant d'Alsace will use a high proportion of Pinot Blanc, which lends flavors of delicate orchard fruits and floral aromas. Other allowed grape varieties include Auxerrois, Pinot Gris, Riesling, Chardonnay, and Pinot Noir.

CRÉMANT DE LOIRE: Crémant de Loire is produced in the Anjou-Saumur and Touraine regions of the Loire Valley. They mostly use Chenin Blanc, but Chardonnay,

Orbois, Cabernet Franc, Grolleau, Pineau d'Aunis, and Pinot Noir are also permitted. They're usually crisp, very fresh and mineral, with quince and hazelnut flavors.

CRÉMANT DE BORDEAUX: Crémant de Bordeaux uses Sauvignon Blanc, Sémillon, and Muscadelle as well as Merlot and Cabernet Sauvignon grapes for their blends. You'll find more floral, grassy aromas in these Crémants.

CRÉMANT DE BOURGOGNE: Crémant de Bourgogne uses Chardonnay and Pinot Noir for their production, with the addition of Gamay as well. The grapes used for the production come from very varied terroirs from the different vineyards of Burgundy and can have expressions ranging from very light, mineral, and zesty to rich and creamy.

CRÉMANT DE JURA: Located near the French border with Switzerland, most of these sparkling wines are made exclusively from Chardonnay, although Pinot Noir and other local grape varieties (Trousseau, Poulsard, and Savagnin) are also used. Jura offers mature and ripe sparkling wines.

CRÉMANT DE SAVOIE: Savoie has a long history of making sparkling wines, but it's the latest region to be allowed within the Crémant exclusive group since 2014. Local varietals Jacquère and Altesse, along with Chardonnay, Pinot Noir, and Gamay, make up the composition. They're delicate and fresh with bright floral notes.

CRÉMANT DE DIE: Die is located in the Southern Rhône region of France. Their Crémants are made with Clairette and Muscat grapes with a very aromatic, perfumed, and bright style.

CRÉMANT DE LIMOUX: Located in Languedoc-Roussillon, Crémant de Limoux must be made from Chardonnay, Chenin Blanc, or Mauzac. The resulting wines are very smooth and creamy.

Good With: Crémants are good with all kinds of canapés and appetizers, poultry, seafood, creamy soups, fresh and earthy vegetables, light fruity desserts, and cheese plates.

Try It with These Recipes: Fig, Camembert & Arugula Flatbreads (page 112); Crab Cakes with Tangerine Salsa (page 158); Tempura Shrimp (page 162); Black Bean & Corn Chilaquiles (page 182)

Also Try: *Cava, Sekt, Blanquette de Limoux*

PROSECCO

Pronunciation: proh·SEHK·koh

Where It's Made: Veneto and Friuli-Venezia-Giula, Italy

Recommended Producers: Nino Franco (Valdobbiadene, Veneto), Bisol (Valdobbiadene, Veneto), Mionetto (Valdobbiadene, Veneto), Villa Sandi (Treviso, Veneto), Carpene Malvolti (Conegliano, Veneto)

Overarching Characteristics: Youthful, light-bodied, aromatic, floral, green almond

Prosecco is by far the most popular sparkling wine. In 2019, 530 million bottles were sold worldwide under the Prosecco label. It's a global phenomenon, mostly attributed to its ready availability, low price, and easy-drinking character. These sparkling wines are made using the Charmat method (page 16), which means they're easy to produce in large quantities, and they can be either **spumante** (fully sparkling) or **frizzante** (slightly sparkling). The main grape variety used in the production is glera.

There are different quality levels of Prosecco following Italian regulatory systems DOC (Denominazione di Origine Controllata) or DOCG (Denominazione di Origine Controllata e Garantita) that are very easy to identify:

- Prosecco DOC is the basic **appellation**.

- Conegliano Valdobbiadene Prosecco Superiore DOCG is a specific location with favorable growing conditions for higher-end Prosecco.

- Asolo Prosecco Superiore DOCG is made on the Colli Asolani hill and distinguishes itself with its salty flavor.

- Prosecco Superiore Rive DOCG designates 43 specific single vineyards in the Conegliano-Valdobiaddene district.

- Prosecco Superiore di Cartizze DOCG refers to a special 107 hectares of remarkably steep vineyards at the highest point of the Valdobbiadene Hill. It is known as the best expression possible.

Prosecco's character is quite precise; it's easily recognizable. Proseccos are quite aromatic and their aromas may include fresh flowers, tangy citrus fruits, orchard fruits, and the very distinctive green almond. Richer expressions may include ripe peach and pear aromas.

Good with: Thai foods, curry, foccacia, egg dishes, mild cheeses, panetonne, souf-
flés, almonds

Try It with These Recipes: Almond Biscotti (page 124), Classic Panettone (page 140),
Black Bean & Corn Chilaquiles (page 182)

Also Try: Moscato d'Asti, pétillant naturel, spumante

CAVA

Pronunciation: KAA·vuh

Where It's Made: Spain, especially in Penedès

Recommended Producers: Raventós i Blanc (Penedès, Catalonia), Juvé y Camps
(Penedès, Catalonia), Agustí Torelló Mata (Penedès, Catalonia), Parés Baltà (Penedès,
Catalonia), Segura Viudas (Penedès, Catalonia)

Overarching Characteristics: Crisp, fine bubbles, complex aromas, orchard
fruits, nutty

Cava comes exclusively from Spain and is made with the traditional method. The
production area spans 10 provinces, but realistically more than 95 percent of
Cavas are made in Penedès, in Catalonia. They're made mostly with three local
grape varieties: Macabeo, which brings bright tropical fruit flavors; Parellada to
provide texture, body, fresh citrus, and nutty notes; and Xarel-lo, which is very tart
and brings a lot of freshness. Other varieties may include Chardonnay, Grenache,
Monastrell, Trepat, and Pinot Noir. Red grape varieties will bring red berries and floral
aromas to a blend. They're often used to produce the rosé Cava.

The sweetness levels of Cava follow the Champagne model, but the different quality
levels are based on aging requirements. The more time spent on lees, the more complex the wine, the more nutty and toasty aromas you get. Basic Cava has a minimum
of 9 months on lees, reserve Cava is 15 months, and gran reserva has a minimum
of 30 months on lees. Additionally, since July 2017, a new qualification named Cava
de Paraje Calificado is now available. These top-range Cavas are single-vineyard,
from the best terroir, and have a minimum aging requirement of 36 months. These
top-tier Cavas can get quite pricey, but most are generally quite affordable.

Good with: Tapas, fried foods, charcuterie, cheese, olives, fried calamari, salads,
citrus flavors, anchovies

Try It with These Recipes: Heirloom Tomato & Peach Bruschetta (page 110), Tempura Shrimp (page 162), Summer Gazpacho with Asiago-Garlic Toast (page 152)

Also Try: Crémant, Sekt, Franciacorta

SEKT

Other Names: Rieslingsekt, Winzersekt

Pronunciation: ZEKT

Where It's Made: Germany and Austria

Recommended Producers: Bründlmayer (Austria), Loimer (Austria), Sekthaus Raumland (Germany), Von Buhl (Germany)

Overarching Characteristics: Bright, tart, dynamic, citrusy, perfumed

Sekt has an exciting flavor profile and has been a revelation for many wine lovers. Germany and Austria have a reputation for high-quality wines with bright acidity, tart citrus fruit, and floral aromas as well as great **minerality**; their cool climate is ideal for sparkling wine production. However, you have to know what to look for as there's a huge quality step between basic German Sekts and good-quality Sekts. A few terms can help you guide your choice.

Most Sekts are German, made with the Charmat method (page 16), like Prosecco. Many of them are fizzy, overly sweet, and the grapes may come in bulk from outside of Germany with no terroir identity. "Deutscher Sekt" indicates that all the grapes were grown in Germany, which is a good start, but they're still not the best expression—far from it. Varieties may include Pinot Blanc, Riesling, Pinot Gris, and Pinot Noir. They're still made with the tank method with high sweetness levels.

If you want quality sparkling wines, you need to look for the term "Sekt b.A." It will specify provenance from one of the 13 official German wine regions (Mosel, Rheinhessen, Pfalz, etc.) and may be made either from the tank method or traditional method. The latter may be labeled as "Klassische Flaschengärung." Germany specializes in Sekt made from Riesling, which is called Rieslingsekt. These sparkling wines are particularly aromatic and perfumed. The best expressions will be labeled as "Winzersekt," which are single-varietal and estate-grown sparkling wines.

Austria also makes some vibrant sparkling wines with local grape varietals. The country has clear regulations concerning bubbles, which are made using mostly Grüner Veltliner as the grape variety. Sekt "Klassik" can be made either from the tank or traditional method. They're rather simple, but very dynamic. Sekt "Reserve" can be made only with the traditional method and have a minimum aging requirement of 18 months on lees. These wines are quite rich and complex with outstanding quality. Sekt "Grösse Reserve" is the best quality Sekt you can get. The aging requirement is 30 months, and the grapes must come from the best vineyards.

Good with: Fish dishes, cooked vegetables, cured meats, sushi

Try It with These Recipes: Bacon-Asiago Popcorn (page 105), Lemony Onion Rings (page 113), Crab Cakes with Tangerine Salsa (page 158), Open-Faced Smoked Salmon Sandwiches (page 165)

Also Try: Finger Lakes sparkling wines, Crémant d'Alsace, Champagne

MOSCATO D'ASTI

Pronunciation: mo·SCAH·toh DAHS·tee

Where It's Made: Piedmont, Italy

Recommended Producers: Michele Chiarlo (Asti, Piedmont), Bera Vittorio e Figli (Asti, Piedmont), Saracco (Asti, Piedmont), La Spinetta (Asti, Piedmont)

Overarching Characteristics: Slightly sparkling, low-alcohol, perfumed, grapey, sweet

As with many Italian appellations, the name alone tells you a lot. Moscato is the grape variety and Asti, a small village in Piedmont, is the production area. Moscato d'Asti is an off-dry, slightly sparkling, low-alcohol wine (5 to 6 percent ABV) with a very charming and aromatic character. It's very floral, grapey, and has fresh peach aromas.

The Piedmont region is known mostly as the home for Nebbiolo, but Moscato d'Asti production is historic. It uses the Martinotti method, also called the Asti method: sparkling from one fermentation only, in a pressurized tank that deliberately releases some of the carbon dioxide. When the wine reaches the right alcohol content, around 5 percent, it is cooled down and the fermentation stops.

In the same area, you may find Asti Spumante, which is slightly different. It's also made from Moscato grapes, but the style is drier, fully sparkling, and has higher alcohol content, around 9 percent ABV.

Good with: Panettone, fruit tarts, pastries made with hazelnuts or almonds, ice cream

Try It with These Recipes: Almond Biscotti (page 124), Key Lime Coconut Pie (page 132), Pear & Orange Dutch Baby (page 148), Black Bean & Corn Chilaquiles (page 182)

Also Try: *Asti Spumante, Californian Moscato, Australian Moscato*

LAMBRUSCO

Pronunciation: lam·BROO·skoh

Where It's Made: Emilia-Romagna, Italy

Recommended Producers: Cleto Chiarli (Modena, Emilia-Romagna), Fattoria Moretto (Modena, Emilia-Romagna), Cantina di Sorbara (Modena, Emilia-Romagna)

Overarching Characteristics: Bright-colored, crisp, structured, fruity

The word "Lambrusco" refers to not only a style of wine, but also a family of native Italian grape varieties. More than 60 Lambrusco varieties have been identified so far. Exclusive to the Emilia-Romagna region of Italy, this sparkling red surprises with its tannic side. They're known as a cheap and fizzy, juice-like beverage; but the truth is the style can range tremendously, from dry to sweet, from lightweight and delicate to heavily structured, from light pink to deep red color. The best expressions are dry, refreshing, and very flavorful. Here are the styles you should be looking for.

Lambrusco di Sorbara: This is the lightest style of Lambrusco, with a very delicate and floral expression. It's light-colored and the most refined of its kind. These wines are dry, but they have fruity aromas of watermelon, mandarin, red berries, cherries, and, of course, many floral notes, but especially of violets.

Lambrusco Grasparossa di Castelvetro: Quite the opposite from Sorbara style, Grasparossa is the heaviest Lambrusco. They're creamy and structured with strong tannins and bold red and black fruit aromas.

Good with: Prosciutto, sausages, bacon, burgers, Thai food, pizza

Try It with These Recipes: Pomegranate-Glazed Turkey Meatballs (page 120), Chocolate Truffle Semifreddo with Toasted Hazelnuts (page 128), Hoisin Chicken Lettuce Wraps (page 164)

Also Try: *Brachetto d'Acqui, sparkling Shiraz, Bugey-Cerdon*

OTHER SPARKLING WINES

As sparkling wines gain popularity, people have started producing them everywhere in the world. These wines all have one thing in common: They love food.

OTHER ITALIAN SPARKLING WINES

Franciacorta is often called the Italian Champagne because this region produces wines using the same traditional method, using Chardonnay, Pinot Noir, and Pinot Blanc with a very elegant style. The appellation itself, in Lombardy, is quite small with only 150 producers, mostly on a small scale.

Other Italian sparkling wines include Trento DOC, which offers fresh, cool-climate bubbles, and Brachetto d'Acqui for sweet sparkling red wines, but almost all Italian wine regions also produces their own sparkling wine that you'll find labeled as "spumante," which just means sparkling.

Good with: Smoked salmon, tuna tartare, risotto, fritto misto, soft-ripened cheeses

Try It with These Recipes: Bacon-Asiago Popcorn (page 105), Crab Cakes with Tangerine Salsa (page 158), Open-Faced Smoked Salmon Sandwiches (page 165)

NEW WORLD SPARKLING WINES

The **New World** is fond of sparkling wines. They're produced everywhere, although regulations are often more lax compared to European producing regions, which makes it harder to link a specific style to a place. You'll always find great sparkling expressions in cooler climates. Think the Finger Lakes in New York, Niagara in Ontario, and Tasmania in Australia.

Good with: Seafood, appetizers, cooked vegetables, fried foods, charcuterie, cheese

Try It with These Recipes: Fig, Camembert & Arugula Flatbreads (page 112); Eggs Benedict with Avocado (page 144); Sautéed Pork Dumplings with Spinach & Sesame (page 166)

OTHER FRENCH SPARKLING WINES

Beyond Crémant and Champagne, France has a lot of sparkling options. In the Loire Valley, you may find Vouvray Mousseux, Saumur Brut, or Montlouis-sur Loire; Blanquette de Limoux in the Languedoc; Saint-Péray, Clairette de Die, and Clairette de Bellegarde in the Rhône Valley; and Bugey-Cerdon in the Savoie. With their fragrant bright pink and luscious sparklings, there's such a wide range of choices.

Good with: Fish, seafood, chicken, charcuterie, snacks and nibbles, dried fruits, fried food, appetizers

Try It with These Recipes: Hoisin Chicken Lettuce Wraps (page 164), Black Bean & Corn Chilaquiles (page 182), Lemony Onion Rings (page 113)

Sweet & Fortified Wines

PORT

Pronunciation: PORT

Where It's Made: Douro Valley, Portugal

Recommended Producers: Ramos Pinto (Vila Nova de Gaia, Portugal), Sandeman (Vila Nova de Gaia, Portugal), Quinta do Noval (Vila Nova de Gaia, Portugal), Niepoort (Vila Nova de Gaia, Portugal)

Overarching Characteristics: Rich, concentrated, luscious, high alcohol, dried fruits, nutty

Port is a fortified wine, which means you can expect a sweet, strong, concentrated, and high-alcohol wine. The fermentation process is stopped midway with the addition of a neutral spirit called aguardente. This also means that the natural sugar in the grape must (crushed grapes going through fermentation) has not yet transformed completely, thus leaving residual sugar in the wine.

Port is the most recognized fortified wine on the planet, thanks to its centuries-old winemaking history and tradition. Port wines use unique local blends of indigenous grape varietals. The most common are Touriga Nacional, Tinta Roriz, Touriga Franca, Tinta Barroca, and Tinta Cão, but there are more than 50 different varietals. These grapes are grown on the extremely steep, hand-terraced, **schist**-rich hills of the Douro River, which has been a UNESCO Heritage Site since 2001.

Port wines can be made in very different styles based on the aging method: either barrel-aged or bottle-aged.

BARREL-AGED STYLES

Barrel-aged Ports are usually ready to drink when released; they won't need any further aging in the bottle. They'll show the most evolved aromas of nuts, caramel, orange, and spices. These are the different barrel-aged styles of Port:

Ruby: Ruby Port is a blend of young wines from multiple vintages. It's the lightest and fruitiest style of Port. Since it's widely available and often produced in bulk, it's also the most affordable. It's an entry-level Port that can also be a good option to cook with.

Tawny: These are blends of old vintages that have been kept in barrels. They'll have an age indication (ranging from 10 to 40 years old) which refers to the average of all the vintages in the blend. Tawny Ports are amber-colored and very rich with a nutty, dried fruit, oxidative, caramel taste.

Colheita: This refers to a barrel-aged tawny style of wine, but from a single vintage. They must be aged in casks for a minimum of seven years.

BOTTLE-AGED STYLES

Bottle-aged Ports are the kind you need to keep for decades before getting their best expression. They're powerful and concentrated and need time to soften and develop further. These are the different bottle-aged styles:

Late-Bottled Vintage (LBV): These wines come from a specific vintage and must be aged in casks for four to six years. This modern style of Port has good aging potential after it's available to purchase. They shouldn't be opened right away, but rather stored for 5 to 10 years.

Vintage: A selection of the best vineyards, made only in the best declared vintages. They're only aged in casks for two years before being bottled, but they're meant to be kept in bottle for at least 15 to 20 years.

Good with: Ruby-style Port pairs well with intense flavors like blue cheese and chocolate-based desserts. Tawny style pairs well with nutty and hard cheeses, apple desserts, caramel, honey, crème brûlée, and foie gras.

Try It with These Recipes: Sweet & Spicy Candied Pecans (page 106), Banana-Cinnamon Bread Pudding (page 123), Chocolate Truffle Semifreddo with Toasted Hazelnuts (page 128), Chocolate-Cherry Flourless Torte (page 136), Grilled Sirloin with Herb & Blue Cheese Compound Butter (page 203), Barbecue Spareribs (page 210)

Also Try: *Vins Doux Naturels, Sherry*

OTHER STYLES OF FORTIFIED WINES

Don't overlook the varied and delicious fortified wines that come from other regions. Here are a few favorites.

MADEIRA

Made exclusively on the Portuguese island of Madeira, this kind of fortified wine undergoes a very special aging period. Historically, Madeira had to be shipped in barrels by boat for months on the seas in tropical conditions. This caused the wine to age prematurely and gave a very oxidized style. Today, aging techniques try to re-create those heated conditions either by estufagem (in heated vats for three months) or canteiro (in a warm room for two years). The style will depend on the grape variety used: Sercial and Verdelho become dry to semidry Madeira, whereas Boal and Malmsey become medium-sweet to sweet styles.

Good with: Spiced cakes, desserts, peanut butter and other nuts, mushrooms, olives, smoked meats

Try It with These Recipes: Sweet & Spicy Candied Pecans (page 106); Sweet Potatoes Stuffed with Sautéed Brussels Sprouts, Cranberries & Cashews (page 190)

SHERRY

Sherry (also called Xérès) is made in the south of Spain in three specific towns: Jerez de la Frontera, El Puerto de Santa María, and Sanlúcar de Barrameda. There are two different styles of Sherry: oxidative and under flor. **Flor** describes the layer of yeast that forms on top of the developing wine. Oxidative styles are the sweetest and most luscious. These include Oloroso, Palo Cortado, Cream, and Pedro Ximénez. Sherry aged under flor will have a dry style, with less alcohol and a savory and saline character. These include Fino, Manzanilla, and Amontillado. Their dryness makes them quite interesting in terms of pairing, and also for cooking.

Good with: The oxidative style pairs well with all kinds of desserts such as brownies, tiramisu, and ice cream as well as braised meats and beef jerky. Under flor, or the dry style, pairs well with shellfish, smoked salmon, nutty cheeses, olive tapenade, onion soup, foie gras, and salty nuts.

Try It with These Recipes: Bacon-Wrapped Dates with Goat Cheese (page 107), Cinnamon Sugar Churros (page 126), Mediterranean-Inspired Pasta Frittata (page 146), Mussels with Parmesan & Herbs (page 195)

VINS DOUX NATURELS

VDNs, also called "Vins Muté," are naturally sweet, fortified wines made in the South of France. They're either made from Grenache (like in the case of Banyuls, Maury, and Rasteau) or from Muscat, which gives a very aromatic style (as in the case of Rivesaltes and Muscat Beaume-de-Venise).

Good with: Grenache-based VDN pairs well with dark chocolate, nuts, and coffee desserts as well as savory terrines and blue cheeses. Muscat-based VDN pairs well with fruity, creamy desserts, pineapples, ricotta, grapefruit, and panna cotta.

Try It with These Recipes: Grenache-based VDN: Chocolate-Cherry Flourless Torte (page 136), Grilled Sirloin with Herb & Blue Cheese Compound Butter (page 203), Barbecue Spareribs (page 210); Muscat-based VDN: Key Lime Coconut Pie (page 132), Pineapple Cheesecake (page 138)

SAUTERNES, BARSAC & ALTERNATIVES

Pronunciation: soh·TEHRN / BAAR·sak

Where It's Made: Bordeaux, France

Recommended Producers: Château Coutet (Barsac, Bordeaux), Château Doisy-Daëne (Sauternes, Bordeaux), Château Climens (Barsac, Bordeaux)

Overarching Characteristics: Mellow, honeyed, cloying, complex, caramel, apricot

Sauternes and Barsac are the two main regions (known as appellations) in Bordeaux producing botrytized (affected by noble rot) sweet wines mostly from Sémillon grapes. These grapes are located in the southwest part of the region, where the Garonne River meets its tributary called Ciron. The crossing of these two rivers creates a very unique microclimate, subject to humid morning fogs and drying, sunny, windy afternoons. These specific conditions are needed for noble rot to develop on the grapes. Also called **botrytis cinerea**, noble rot is a type of fungus that makes the grapes shrivel. Noble rot concentrates and sweetens the wine, and gives it intense aromas of honey, beeswax, dried fruit, caramel, and sweet spices.

Other areas within Bordeaux also produce sweet botrytised wines, including Cérons, Sainte-Croix-du-Mont, Cadillac, Loupiac, Premières Côtes de Bordeaux, Côtes de Bordeaux Saint-Macaire, and Monbazillac. These offer similar profiles while being way more affordable.

Noble rot is not in any way exclusive to Bordeaux, as we can find some sweet, delicious gold liquids all over. Tokaj wines in Hungary are extremely expressive and delicious. German Beerenauslese and Trockenbeerenauslese Rieslings are also (deliciously) shriveled and moldy. In Loire, botrytized wines from Chenin Blanc are made in Coteaux du Layon, Bonnezeaux, and Quart de Chaume. In Alsace, they're called **Sélection de Grains Nobles** (SGN). Austria has their famous Ausbruch in the town of Rust as well as their own Beerenauslese and Trockenbeerenauslese.

Good with: Foie gras, cheeses, light desserts, fruit tarts, cream- and custard-based desserts, cheesecake, cured meats

Try It with These Recipes: Pineapple Cheesecake (page 138), Tarte Tatin (page 134), Coffee Crème Brûlée (page 130)

Also Try: *Tokaj, Sélection de Grains Nobles, late harvest*

OTHER SWEET WINES

Sweet wines can vary in flavor and expression, and it's worth trying several.

LATE HARVEST

Late harvest is pretty much self-explanatory. You leave the grapes longer on the vine and they continue to mature, grow more concentrated in flavor, and eventually start to dry out and become raisins. In Alsace and throughout France, they're called Vendanges Tardives. Late-harvest wines are also popular in the New World, especially in Argentina, Chile, California, and Australia. They get very concentrated flavors of caramel, stone fruits, and tropical fruits as well as a very creamy, luscious mouthfeel.

One noted example is Vin de Constance, an iconic sweet wine from South Africa that has been produced for more than 300 years by Klein Constantia, that's made from Muscat grapes. Young Vin de Constance will show delicate nougat aromas with fruity notes of orange zest and exotic fruits. Rich and complex, it can age into decadent masterpieces.

Good with: Foie gras, cheesecake, pad Thai, fruit-filled pastries, prosciutto

Try It with These Recipes: Sweet & Spicy Candied Pecans (page 106), Banana-Cinnamon Bread Pudding (page 123), Tarte Tatin (page 134), Pineapple Cheesecake (page 138)

ICE WINES

To make ice wines, you must leave grapes on the vines to freeze when the temperature drops below -17°F. If the temperature drop happens too late in the growing season, the grapes may fall and rot. If it happens too early, before perfect maturity has been reached, the grapes will be damaged and lost. Canada is the king of ice wines. Germany has a long history of eiswein making, too, but the last decade has proven to be difficult with warm winters. Ice wines are heavily sweet with luscious body. Aromas are quite rich and concentrated with hints of honey and cooked orchard fruits.

Good with: Apricots, banana pudding, custard, melon

Try It with These Recipes: Banana-Cinnamon Bread Pudding (page 123), Tarte Tatin (page 134)

PASSITO

Passito, also called **appassimento**, is a process used when grapes are laid on either straw mats or crates, or hung to dry. These wines have rich and complex aromas of nuts, dried figs, dates, and molasses. In Italy, you may find these wines under the name Vin Santo. This process is also used for Greek Vin Santo as well as German Strohwein, Austrian Schilfwein, and French Vin de Paille. Red and white local grapes may be used.

Good With: Biscotti, fruit tarts, game birds, grapes, pumpkin pie, bacon, glazed ham

Try It with These Recipes: Bacon-Wrapped Dates with Goat Cheese (page 107), Almond Biscotti (page 124)

White & Rosé Wines

CRISP & EDGY WHITES

AROMATIC WHITES

RICH & BOLD WHITES

ROSÉ WINES

Know Your White Wine

If we go back a few years, red wines were undoubtedly more popular than whites. However, there has been a recent shift in white wine consumption, and one of the main reasons is directly linked to food trends. As health is clearly the focus now, vegetables are taking the center stage and our meals tend to be lighter, so the wines needed to adapt. Lightness, lower alcohol content, diminished sweetness, delicate flavors, and portion size are all gaining momentum in food and beverages. Overall, white wines are easier to pair than reds. Think of any place with a great seafood culture, near the Mediterranean or Atlantic coast, for example, and white wine will always take an important place on the table.

In any wines, you are looking for three kinds of aromas and flavors. First, you have the primary aromas, which are basically anything fruity or floral. Primary aromas are the pure expression of the grapes. Then, there are secondary aromas that are the results of vinification methods. The fermentation itself can be responsible for some aromas such as spices, mushrooms, and beer. Secondary aromas also include anything related to oak aging after fermentation. French oak will give vanilla and clove aromas, whereas American oak is known for roasted coconut, sweet spices, and charred wood notes.

Another process that can lend a specific flavor is **malolactic** fermentation. This describes the transformation of malic acid into lactic acid, which typically occurs while wine ages in barrels. This gives the wine a buttery flavor as well as a creamy texture. This step is mandatory in every red wine, but can be either skipped or partially or fully completed for white wines. Crisp & Edgy Whites (page 43) will normally have very little intervention, whereas Rich & Bold Whites (page 62) most probably undergo oak treatment or malolactic treatment. Finally, a tertiary aroma comes from aging. As the wine ages, it will lose its fruity primary aromas to transform into evolved notes such as truffles, leather, tobacco, and smoke.

EVERYTHING YOU NEED TO KNOW
ABOUT ORANGE WINE

Sometimes mistakenly put in the same category as natural wines, orange wines are quite different. In fact, organic and eco-friendly production is not even part of their criteria. The name can be misleading as there's no actual orange in the wine and the color's not always orange-tinted. It's more of a copper hue, really. I prefer the term "skin macerated," which is more evocative (and honest). They're simply white wines made like red wines: wines that are left for a while to macerate with the skins and seeds. Orange wine's history dates back to antiquity and it has a very attractive and unique aromatic profile. They have a bitter, sour, very savory taste with aromas from the oxidation such as nuts and dried orange. They tend to have high acidity and low alcohol but also a robust and tannic structure. Indeed, white wines can have tannins, and orange wines are the perfect example; although the tannins in orange wines will be more subtle than, say, a bold Cabernet Sauvignon. Orange wines can be a fun and audacious choice for pairing. Don't be shy—try this wine with nuts, Indian butter chicken, various kinds of cheeses, hot sauce, or anything with cardamom, saffron, or cinnamon, and so much more. It's the perfect in-between red and white!

Know Your Rosé

Summer wouldn't be the same without rosé. The freshness and aromatic profile make it perfect for picnic foods such as sandwiches, salads, lobster rolls, and even hot dogs. But did you know you're allowed to drink pink wines all year long?

As it happens, there are four different ways to make rosé. The most widespread is **maceration** rosé. Color comes from the skin of the grapes. So, these kinds of rosés are made exactly like red wines, except they're left on their skin for a shorter amount of time. Another technique is called direct pressing. Used to produce the lightest styles of rosé, direct pressing doesn't leave time for maceration. The grapes are pressed directly, and the contact with the skin is very limited. **Saignée method**, also called bleeding, is a by-product of red wines. While producing a red wine, a producer might decide during maceration to extract some of the juice. The result is a more concentrated red wine, and a rosé on the side. This doesn't mean saignée rosés are lower quality. They actually tend to be richer, with intense fruity flavors. Blending is also allowed in some places in the world. By mixing red with white wine—you guessed it—you get rosé. The only region in Europe allowed to use blending is Champagne, but we can also find some blended rosés in the New World.

Crisp & Edgy Whites

MUSCADET

Other Names: Melon de Bourgogne, Melon

Pronunciation: MUH·skuh·dei

Where It's Made: Pays Nantais in the Loire region of France

Recommended Producers: Domaine Pierre Luneau-Papin (Loire, France), Domaine de l'Ecu (Loire, France), Lieubeau (Loire, France), Guilbaud Frères (Loire, France), Sauvion (Loire, France)

Overarching Characteristics: Neutral, saline, delicate, light-bodied, citrus aromas

Muscadet is a soft and delicate wine, quite shy in terms of aromas, but it shows all its beauty in its rounded texture. It's a wine that is full of subtlety, and that is exactly the reason it can successfully show beautiful minerality and iodine character that are so often overpowered by other aromas in most wines. It shouldn't be mistaken for Muscat even if the names are similar—they're quite opposites in every way.

Nantes, in the most western part of the Loire Valley with proximity to the ocean, is home to Muscadet, and to some of France's finest oysters, like the popular Gillardeau, which are plump, briny, and too big for one bite. Its proximity to the strong sea breezes is what gives Muscadet its saline character, and makes it a natural match for shellfish.

Muscadet wines are often aged on lees, as indicated on the labels with the French term "sur lie." This means the wine has been left for an extended period of time on the dead yeast cells from fermentation. This technique gives richness, texture, and yeasty character to the wines. Muscadet Sèvre-et-Maine, along with its three recognized Crus, Le Pallet, Clisson, and Gorges, is the most recognized appellation for the superior quality of their Muscadets.

Good with: Oysters, mussels, snails, seafood, tofu, beurre blanc sauce, delicate fish, and Swiss cheese

Try It with These Recipes: Tempura Shrimp (page 162), Mussels with Parmesan & Herbs (page 195), Broiled Oysters with Gremolata (page 163)

Also Try: *Pinot Blanc, Aligoté, Auxerrois, Piquepoul, Sylvaner, Chablis*

VERDICCHIO

Other Names: Trebbiano di Soave, Trebbiano di Lugana, Trebbiano Valtenesi, Marchigiano, Turbiana

Pronunciation: vehr·DEE·kee·oh

Where It's Made: Marche, Italy

Recommended Producers: Bucci (Marche, Italy), Umani Ronchi (Marche, Italy), Podium Garofoli (Marche, Italy), Velenosi (Marche, Italy)

Overarching Characteristics: Light, easy drinking, grapefruit, peach, tart, oily

Verdicchio's home is in the Central Italian region of Marche, along the Adriatic Coast. It is mostly known as two appellations, Verdicchio dei Castelli di Jesi and Verdicchio di Matelica. Verdicchio is often vinified as a single-varietal, but may also be blended with Malvasia and Trebbiano. It makes high-acidity, light, and refreshing wines with herbaceous, tart citrus and grapefruit flavors as well as stone fruit in warmer areas. Verdicchio is quite lean but has a great oily texture which gives it complexity. In its best expression you can also get delicious almond flavors. It's a good aperitive wine to start a meal and often very affordable. For the full Marchigiano experience, try Verdicchio with ascoli olives, a regional treat of meat-stuffed olives that are breaded and deep-fried.

Good with: Salads, vegetables, quiche, almonds, seafood, ascoli olives

Try It with These Recipes: Shrimp Ceviche with Cucumber & Avocado (page 109); Garlic-Parmesan Roasted Edamame (page 104); Summer Gazpacho with Asiago-Garlic Toast (page 152); Crunchy Chopped Vegetable Tabbouleh (page 174); Panfried Trout with Brown Butter, Dill & Fingerling Potatoes (page 200); Beet Ravioli with Ricotta Cheese, Orange, Pistachio & Parsley (page 186)

Also Try: Sauvignon Blanc, Albariño, Grüner Veltliner, Verdejo

SAUVIGNON BLANC

Other Names: Sauvignon, **Fumé Blanc**, Sauvignon Bianco, Muskat-Silvaner, Muskat-Sylvaner, Feigentraube

Pronunciation: SO·vee·nyohn BLAHN, although it is often pronounced with a hard "K" from English speaker: SO·vee·nyohn BLAHNK

Where It's Made: France (Loire, Bordeaux), California, New Zealand, Australia, South Africa, Italy (Friuli, Alto Adige), and more

Recommended Producers: Henri Bourgeois (Sancerre, Loire), Craggy Range (Marlborough, New Zealand), Klein Constantia (South Africa), Château Smith Haut Lafitte (Pessac-Léognan, Bordeaux), Robert Mondavi (Oakville, California)

Overarching Characteristics: Crisp, dry, aromatic, simple, herbaceous, versatile, citrus-forward

Sauvignon Blanc is simply one of the most versatile and straightforward grape varieties, especially in terms of pairing. These green-skinned grapes are relatively easy to grow and the wine's typical high-acidity profile makes it particularly food-friendly.

It's generally crisp, dry, aromatic, and extremely distinctive—the very definition of thirst-quenching. The grapes often feature citrus fruits, gooseberries, a strong herbaceous character, and the occasional "cat's pee," a funky, tangy aroma associated with this varietal. In warmer climates, riper and more intense flavors of passion fruit or peach emerge. Sauvignon Blanc wines are relatively simple, quite similar wherever they are produced, and are one of the most easily recognizable. Their bold, green character is remarkable with green vegetables, tomatoes, and salads.

Sauvignon Blanc was historically associated with two specific regions in France: Bordeaux and the Loire Valley. Some of the best examples of Sauvignon Blanc can be found in the eastern part of the Loire Valley, especially in Sancerre and Pouilly-Fumé. Sancerre wines are especially recognized in association with the famous Crottin de Chavignol goat cheese, which is a celebrated pairing. The wines of the Loire Valley are closely linked to the terroir. They'll have distinctive flinty, smoky aromas that may surprise you when you open the bottle. However, anytime the term "fumé" is used (as in Pouilly-Fumé in the Loire, or fumé blanc in California), this indicates oak aging and a bold, rich style quite different from the vibrant young expressions. Bordeaux-based Sauvignon Blanc are typically blended with Sémillon and muscadelle, and in some cases, they may also have some oak aging.

Outside France, the variety has been relatively successful in the New World. New Zealand, California, and South Africa have thriving vineyards. Nowadays, it is the third-most-planted white grape in the world, and one of the most widespread international varieties.

Good with: Salads, vegetarian dishes, vegetables (asparagus, cucumbers, eggplant), herbs, delicate fish, seafood, fresh cheeses

Try It with These Recipes: Shrimp Ceviche with Cucumber & Avocado (page 109); Caramelized Onion Tart with Feta Cheese & Pine Nuts (page 111); Eggs Benedict with Avocado (page 144); Garlic-Parmesan Roasted Edamame (page 104); Summer Gazpacho with Asiago-Garlic Toast (page 152); Broiled Oysters with Gremolata (page 163); Crunchy Chopped Vegetable Tabbouleh (page 174); Panfried Trout with Brown Butter, Dill & Fingerling Potatoes (page 200)

Also Try: *Verdicchio, Albariño, Grüner Veltliner*

VERDEJO

Other Names: Verdeja, Albillo de Nava, Botón de Gallo Blanco, Boto de Ball, Cepa de Madrigal, Gouvelo, Verdal del País

Pronunciation: ver·DAY·ho

Where It's Made: Spain, especially in the central region of Rueda

Recommended Producers: Belondrade (Rueda, Spain), Bodegas Ramón Bilbao (Rioja and Rueda, Spain), Bodegas Naia (Rueda, Spain), Telmo Rodríguez (Spain), Viñedos de Nieva (Rueda, Spain)

Overarching Characteristics: Tangy, crisp, and lean, with lemon, lime, and grassy qualities

Native of Central Spain, in a land where red wines have all the spotlight, the Rueda appellation most recognized for their Verdejo production is a drop of white in a sea of red. This crisp, unoaked wine is often blended with other similarly light and zesty varieties such as Sauvignon Blanc, Viura, Macabeo, and Palomino, although Verdejo must make at least 85 percent of the blend, at least for Rueda DO. Verdejo is found in all of Castilla-León as well as in Extremadura, to the south closer to the Portuguese border. Besides Spain, Verdejo is found on a smaller scale in Australia as well as California.

Its name is inspired by the color of the grapes, which are quite green even when they reach complete maturity, as well as the color of the wines, which are slightly green-tinted, especially when young. The wines are palate-pleasing with lemon, lime, melon, and grassy aromas, and sometimes a touch of honey. They're lean and refreshing, especially when produced in altitude like in Rueda where vines are often planted at 600 to 700 meters above sea level.

Good with: Salted vegetables, fish tacos, citrusy sauces and marinades, ricotta, feta, fresh herbs

Try It with These Recipes: Garlic-Parmesan Roasted Edamame (page 104), Shrimp Ceviche with Cucumber & Avocado (page 109), Summer Gazpacho with Asiago-Garlic Toast (page 152)

Also Try: Sauvignon Blanc, Pinot Grigio, Loureiro

GRÜNER VELTLINER

Other Names: Grüner, GrüVe, Veltliner, Grüner Muskateller, Weißgipfler, Veltlin, Veltínskè Zelené, Zöld Veltlini

Pronunciation: GREW·ner velt·LEE·ner

Where It's Made: Austria

Recommended Producers: Domäne Wachau (Wachau, Austria), Weingut Knoll (Wachau, Austria), Weingut Jurtschitsch (Kamptal, Austria), Schloss Gobelsburg (Kamptal, Austria), Weingut Fred Loimer (Langenlois, Austria), Weingut Bründlmayer (Langenlois, Austria), Malat (Kremstal, Austria), Winzer Krems (Kremstal, Austria)

Overarching Characteristics: Zesty, white pepper, high acidity, full-bodied, precise

The Austrian flagship grape variety, Grüner Veltliner, may seem hard to pronounce, but it's definitely easy to love. It is the most planted varietal and quite widespread around the country, but they really stand out in the appellations north of Vienna: Wachau, Kremstal, Kamptal, Wagram, and Weinviertel. If you ever go to Vienna, find a heurigen. These wine taverns, traditionally located on the outskirts of the city near the vineyards, serve local wines with the traditional sizable schnitzel.

Grüner can be quite lean and light when produced from high yields, but its best expressions are rich, full-bodied with brightness, and textural with lovely white pepper aromas. As it ripens quite late, Grüner is great at maintaining high levels of acidity. This, along with its mineral character and ripe fruit flavors, makes it friendly at the table. Its spicy character and bold palate mean it can hold up to richer plates, whereas its high acidity and zesty side makes it a fit with lighter dishes.

Even though it's associated with Austria, Grüner Veltliner is also found in Hungary, Germany, Slovakia, and the Czech Republic as well as North America, Australia, and Northern Italy.

Good with: Asparagus, artichokes, salads, goat cheese, schnitzel

Try It with These Recipes: Eggs Benedict with Avocado (page 144), Open-Faced Smoked Salmon Sandwiches (page 165), Summer Gazpacho with Asiago-Garlic Toast (page 152)

Also Try: *Riesling, Chardonnay, Müller-Thurgau*

PINOT GRIS / PINOT GRIGIO

Other Names: Grauburgunder, Rülander, Grauer Burgunder, Malvoisie, Fromenteau Gris, Pinot Beurot, Auvernat Gris, Auxerrois Gris, and Tokay d'Alsace (but the latter was forbidden in 2007)

Pronunciation: PEE·noh GREE / PEE·noh GREE·jo

Where It's Made: Alsace, Northern Italy—especially Veneto, Trentino, Friuli-Venezia Giulia, Alto Adige—and Germany

Recommended Producers: Domaine Zind-Humbrecht (Alsace), Schlumberger (Alsace), Elena Walch (Alto Adige), Alois Lageder (Alto Adige), Mezzacorona (Trentino)

Overarching Characteristics: Citrus, orchard fruit, honeysuckle, restrained acidity, softness

Pinot Gris, or Pinot Grigio, isn't exactly a white grape. The clusters of berries boast a lovely shade of pink varying from dark, brownish pink to dusty copper. It's part of the big Pinot family and a mutation of Pinot Noir.

Pinot Gris is often described as a crowd-pleaser, as it suits many palates. It is soft and doesn't have a marked acidity, and it can be either light- or full-bodied, all depending on the ripeness of the grapes when picked. Its aromas can vary from perfumed or neutral with notes of pears, apples, stone fruit, tropical fruit, and even a hint of smoke or wet wool.

Pinot Gris can be found in different styles, from dry to lusciously sweet, as in the extravagant Sélection de Grains Nobles or Vendanges Tardives of Alsace. Pinot Gris and Pinot Grigio are the exact same grape varietal; the name has just been translated (one is French, the other Italian). However, there's evident variation between them because of aspects such as climate, soils, and yields. Italian Pinot Grigios are on the crisp and light side, whereas in the dry Alsatian climate, it gets more maturity, weight, and higher alcohol levels, which translates into a more aromatic profile and heavier body.

Plantings of Pinot Grigio have grown with its popularity, with growers cultivating it from Oregon and California to New Zealand and Australia.

Good with: Depending on the style of the wine and sweetness level, pairings may vary from light salads, pastas, and delicate fish to creamy sauce, poultry, and even fruit-based desserts.

Try It with These Recipes: Heirloom Tomato & Peach Bruschetta (page 110); Pull-Apart Garlic, Parmesan & Herb Bread (page 154); Shoyu-Style Ramen (page 180); Maple-Roasted Parsnips with Pumpkin Seeds (page 175); Beet Ravioli with Ricotta Cheese, Orange, Pistachio & Parsley (page 186); Coconut-Curry Halibut en Papillote (page 202)

Also Try: *Chardonnay, Chenin Blanc, Pinot Blanc, Jurançon*

GARGANEGA

Other Names: Soave, d'Oro, Garganego

Pronunciation: gar·GAH·neh·gah

Where It's Made: Soave in Veneto, but also Puglia and Sicily

Recommended Producers: Bertani (Soave, Veneto), Pieropan (Soave, Veneto), Inama (Soave, Veneto), Prà (Soave, Veneto)

Overarching Characteristics: Floral, apricot, steely, lean

Garganega is one of the most important grape varieties in Italy as well as one of the oldest. It is almost exclusively grown in Veneto, with about 95 percent of total plantings located in the region. You've probably already tasted Garganega without even realizing it. The main appellation responsible for its production, Soave, never names the grape on its labels. It may be blended with other local white grapes, but its best expressions are mostly 100 percent Garganega.

Soave wines are perfumed with floral notes, baked apples, toasted almonds, apricot, and mandarin aromas as well as some steely minerality. It is lean and dry with moderate acidity but a rich texture. Garganega vines can be quite vigorous and achieve high yield; for this reason, it is sometimes mass-produced and quite bland. However, the best producers are able to get great expressions with finesse and concentrated flavors. Soave Classico and Soave Superiore offer both refinement and complexity.

The growing region's proximity to Adriatic also accounts for the wine's affinity to seafood. There's nothing quite like folpi alla veneziana, a traditional Venetian appetizer of octopus, cuttlefish eggs, and shrimp with a squeeze of lemon and a good bottle of Soave.

Good with: Rich pasta sauce, seafood, risotto, herbs, bread, polenta, green vegetables, prosciutto, squash

Try It with These Recipes: Grilled Fruit Caprese Salad (page 149); Pull-Apart Garlic, Parmesan & Herb Bread (page 154); Beet Ravioli with Ricotta Cheese, Orange, Pistachio & Parsley (page 186); Coconut-Curry Halibut en Papillote (page 202)

Also Try: Chenin Blanc, Albariño, Cortese, Malvasia

DOURO WHITES

Pronunciation: DOOR·oh

Where It's Made: Portugal

Recommended Producers: Poças (Douro), Casa Ferreirinha (Douro), Quinta do Vallado (Douro), Niepoort (Douro)

Overarching Characteristics: Refreshing, affordable, zesty, apricot

Portuguese producers have such a wide palette of unique, local grape varietals to choose from—no wonder blends are the norm. Did you know there's a total of 250 Portuguese grapes varieties? The hot, terraced, Douro Valley, historically recognized for its Port wine production, is rapidly increasing its still wine production and can't seem to keep up with the demand. You need to look beyond those valleys to find whites. It's at the top of the hills, where temperatures are fresher, that white grapes are planted.

Some notable grape varieties used are Gouveio, Malvasia, Viosinho, and Rabigato. The wines have a tight acidity from the fresh breeze, a strong mineral character from the hard schistose soils, and fine structure. Aromas are zesty with citrus fruits as well as pear and apricot. More often than not, the wines are aged in neutral oak to give them a smooth palate. This rich character makes them natural partners for strong-flavored fish such as the traditional Portuguese bacalhau, which are salt cod fritters.

Good with: Buttery flavors, fish, salt cod, seafood, octopus

Try It with These Recipes: Creamy Carrot & Ginger Soup (page 153), Falafel with Tzatziki Sauce (page 156), Seared Scallops with Garlic-Basil Butter (page 194)

Also Try: *Alentejo, Lisboa, White Rioja*

ASSYRTIKO

Other Names: Assyrtico or Asyrtiko

Pronunciation: a·seer·TEE·ko

Where It's Made: Santorini, Greece

Recommended Producers: Domaine Sigalas (Santorini, Greece), Boutari Winery (Santorini, Greece), Estate Argyros (Santorini, Greece), Hatzidakis Winery (Santorini, Greece), Gaia Wines (Santorini, Greece)

Overarching Characteristics: Mineral, citrus-forward, dynamic

Assyrtiko, native to Greece, can be found on the island of Santorini in the Aegean Sea. The vines are planted in a unique, traditional manner called Kouloura, or basket-trained. That means they're woven into wreaths close to the ground that resemble little nests. The technique is used to protect the vines from the fierce sea winds, but it also affects the yield—though the vineyards produce very little wine, they make for gorgeous scenery. The island also has rich volcanic soils that provide distinctive mineral character to the wines.

Assyrtiko produces dynamic wines full of character, with high acidity and alcohol levels. It's the perfect match for your favorite Greek salad, which needs this level of acidity to balance the copious amount of feta and olives. Another characteristic of Assyrtiko is that it's susceptible to oxidation. This means producers of still wines will be very careful during vinification and opt for stainless steel instead of barrels.

Good with: Delicate fish and seafood

Try It with These Recipes: Grilled Fruit Caprese Salad (page 149), Falafel with Tzatziki Sauce (page 156)

Also Try: Sémillon, Riesling, Roditis, Moschofilero

ALBARIÑO

Other Names: Alvarinho, Albarina, Alvarin Blanco, Alvarinha, Azal Blanco, Galego, Galeguinho

Pronunciation: ahl·bah·REEN-yo

Where It's Made: Rías Baixas, Spain and Vinho Verde, Portugal

Recommended Producers: Anselmo Mendes (Vinho Verde, Portugal), Quinta de Soalheiro (Vinho Verde, Portugal), Nora da Neve (Rías Baixas, Spain), Adega Pazos (Rías Baixas, Spain), Lagar de Cervera (Rías Baixas, Spain)

Overarching Characteristics: Crisp, nectarine, grapefruit, plump, textured

Albariño and Alvarinho (the former in Spanish, the latter in Portuguese) are the same grape found in the north of the Iberian Peninsula, on either side of the Portuguese-Spanish border. It makes a lightweight wine with vibrant acidity and aromas of nectarine, grapefruit, raw almonds, and a pleasant saline and zesty character. The palate, however, has weight to it. It's full-bodied and can even be waxy. This comes from the thick skin that gives the wine structure and what we call a phenolic component, a slight bitter mouthfeel that almost feel like little tannins.

Rías Baixas, in the northwest of Spain, is the first producing area for Albariño. Galician Albariño tends to have higher stone fruit and melon aromas while maintaining a bright acidity, saline minerality, and interesting body structure. However, the region is separated into five subregions with slightly different styles. You'll find the most melony character in Val do Salnés, a soft style with mainly peach aromas in O Rosa, and savory notes in Condado do Tea.

Its Portuguese twin, Alvarinho, is found right across the border in the northern part of Vinho Verde. It's often used in blends along with other local grape varieties such as Loureiro and Arinto, but more producers tend to embrace its identity as a single-varietal, especially in the subregion of Monção e Melgaço.

Good with: Seafood, risotto, poultry, grilled fish tacos, fried cod cakes, tabbouleh, all kinds of salads

Try It with These Recipes: Garlic-Parmesan Roasted Edamame (page 104); Creamy Coleslaw with Jicama (page 150); Pull-Apart Garlic, Parmesan & Herb Bread (page 154); Pizza Margherita (page 184)

Also Try: Riesling, Avesso, Sémillon, Furmint

CHENIN BLANC

Other Names: Pineau de la Loire, Steen, Pineau d'Anjou

Pronunciation: SHEN·in BLAHN

Where It's Made: Across the Loire Valley and other regions of France, South Africa, Australia, California

Recommended Producers: Vincent Carême (Vouvray, Loire), François Chidaine (Montlouis-sur-Loire, Loire), Domaine Huet (Vouvray, Loire), Ken Forrester (Stellenbosch, South Africa), Beaumont (Overberg, South Africa), Opstal Estate (Western Cape, South Africa)

Overarching Characteristics: Versatile, bone-dry to luscious and sweet, straw, mineral, chamomile, honey

Chenin Blanc has a superpower: It can shape-shift and is so versatile that it can be used to create any style of wine. From amazing sparkling wines, to bone-dry light wines, to heavier oak-aged whites, to some of the most decadent dessert wines in the world, Chenin Blanc is extremely underrated.

Chenin Blanc's most recognized provenance is in the Middle Loire Valley, in a multitude of different appellations between Anjou and Touraine. Savennières wines are associated with strong mineral flavors that are unmistakable; Vouvray has some great dry, off-dry, and sparkling options; Anjou, Saumur, and Touraine can make about any style possible; Quart de Chaume, Coteaux du Layon, Bonnezeaux, and Coulée de Serrant are the masters of the sweets.

However, the biggest Chenin Blanc producer is South Africa, where it's called Steen. Historically, it was planted there for its productivity potential, to be used in bulk wines and brandy. Nowadays, quality is the focus, especially in Stellenbosch. The combination of old bush vines of Chenin and dynamic, ambitious producers have proven to be successful. South African Steens tend to be more tropical than Loire versions with aromas of guava, melon, and banana.

Good with: Dry style pairs well with oysters, trout, eggplant, and shrimp. Off-dry pairs well with spicy dishes, Thai food, citrus tart, peach cobbler, and soft cheeses. Sweet style pairs with decadent cream-based desserts. Sparkling can go with just about anything.

Try It with These Recipes: Tempura Shrimp (page 162), Creamy Coleslaw with Jicama (page 150), Green Mango Salad with Peanut Sauce (page 151), Seared Scallops with Garlic-Basil Butter (page 194)

Also Try: Torrontés, Sémillon, Roussanne, Grenache Blanc

WHITE RIOJA

Other Names: Rioja Blanco

Pronunciation: ree·OH·yuh

Where It's Made: Rioja, Spain

Recommended Producers: Viña Tondonia (Rioja, Spain), Izadi (Rioja, Spain), Marqués de Murrieta (Rioja, Spain)

Overarching Characteristics: Light, lemon, honeydew, smooth, caramelized when aged

Rioja is mostly known for its full-bodied heavy reds, but they also produce some fresh white blends mostly composed of Viura, also called Macabeo, a local variety also used in Cava production. Other grapes allowed in the blend include any of the following: Malvasía, Garnacha Blanca, Tempranillo Blanco, Maturana Blanca, Chardonnay, Sauvignon Blanc, and Verdejo.

The flavor profile of White Rioja depends mainly on its aging period. Joven Rioja means "young." It will have less than 15 months of aging and no oak requirements. Young Riojas are light and crisp with notes of lemon and honeydew, and very little body. Crianza White Rioja has a minimum of 12 months of aging, 6 in oak casks. The requirement increases to 24 months for Reserva and 48 months for Gran Reserva. Aged Riojas will be much heavier with notes of caramel, dried fruits, praline, and nuts. It gets velvety and smooth as it ages.

Good with: Tapas or pintxos, cured meats, grilled fish, canned sardines, strong cheeses

Try It with These Recipes: Summer Gazpacho with Asiago-Garlic Toast (page 152); Panfried Trout with Brown Butter, Dill & Fingerling Potatoes (page 200)

Also Try: *Vermentino, Albariño, Chardonnay*

LANGUEDOC-ROUSSILLON BLENDS

Pronunciation: LAHN·guh·doc ROO·see·yohn

Where It's Made: Languedoc-Roussillon, France

Recommended Producers: Château Rives-Blanques (Limoux, France), Château La Liquière (Faugères, France), Domaine Olivier Pithon (Calce, France), Domaine de la Rectorie (Banyuls, France)

Overarching Characteristics: Mineral-driven, coastal, fresh and structured, concentrated flavors

In far Southern France, near the Spanish Border, Languedoc-Roussillon is a hidden treasure. A Mediterranean paradise during the summer, and a wild, desert, arid, windy area during winter. It's a big wine-producing region in terms of volume, in fact the largest in France, but most of it is red. It's only recently that the region discovered an interest in whites. The local varieties Picpoul, Terret, Clairette, and Grenache

Gris are now finding their place along with Grenache Blanc, Bourboulenc, Rolle, Maccabéo, Marsanne, and Roussanne.

Most of the white production is concentrated on the coastal areas, which brings a vibrant freshness to the wines and often a zesty, saline character. They won't always be blends; single-varietals are also gaining popularity. For example, Picpoul de Pinet has its own appellation, but it's the kind of place where you can find some little gems for very affordable prices.

Good with: Shrimp, Mediterranean salads, seafood, oysters

Try It with These Recipes: Heirloom Tomato & Peach Bruschetta (page 110), Grilled Fruit Caprese Salad (page 149)

Also Try: *Vermentino, Torrontés, Douro Whites, Clairette*

Aromatic Whites

JURANÇON SEC

Pronunciation: JU·rahn·sohn SEK

Where It's Made: Southwest of France

Recommended Producers: Clos Lapeyre (Jurançon, France), Domaine Cauhapé (Jurançon, France), Château Jolys (Jurançon, France)

Overarching Characteristics: Rich, golden, savory, waxy, grapefruit

The Southwest of France has all kinds of small, very niche wine appellations, most of them following Bordeaux styles, but some that are quite unique. Jurançon is one of them. It is the land of Gros Manseng, Petit Manseng, and Petit Courbu wines, either dry (sec), or moelleux (sweet). The blends of both Mansengs are deep gold and rich with fruity flavors like grapefruit, lemon, and pears, and sometimes with spicy nuances. When Petit Manseng is used in a higher ratio, wines will have a savory aspect, with notes of wax.

Good with: Shrimp, grilled salmon, cheese fondue, quiche, crab

Try It with These Recipes: Open-Faced Smoked Salmon Sandwiches (page 165); Classic Lobster Bisque (page 160); Fig, Camembert & Arugula Flatbreads (page 112); Seared Scallops with Garlic-Basil Butter (page 194)

Also Try: *Viognier, Riesling, Sémillon*

RIESLING

Other Names: Weisser Riesling, Johannisberg Riesling, Rhine Riesling

Pronunciation: REE·slihng

Where It's Made: Germany, Austria, Alsace, Australia, New York

Recommended Producers: Trimbach (Alsace, France), Marc Kreydenweiss (Alsace, France), S.A. Prüm (Mosel, Germany) Schloss Johannisberg (Rheinhessen, Germany), Egon Müller (Mosel, Germany), Hermann J. Wiemer (Finger Lakes, United States)

Overarching Characteristics: Perfumed, aromatic, fresh, lime, petrol

Riesling is a star—a sommelier's favorite and a palate pleaser. Its ability to express terroir combined to its refreshing acidity, ageability, and aromatic character makes it unique and very recognizable. These vibrant wines offer plenty of fruity aromas like orchard fruit and apricot, but also some surprising smells of key lime pie, honeycomb, and petrol, especially in older vintages.

As appreciated as it is by connoisseurs, Riesling is still subject to prejudice. It's often misjudged as a sweet, simple wine, when that couldn't be further from the truth. Most Rieslings are exceptional, fine, dry, mouthwatering delights. Indeed, traditionally sweetness was used to balance its high acidity and still is in some styles of Rieslings, but that is easily identifiable on the label.

German Rieslings use the **Prädikatswein** system to identify the style of their wines. This scale is based on the must weight at harvest and not the actual sweetness level, but it still gives a good understanding. Kabinett is always dry, Spätlese can be either dry or off-dry, and then Auslese, Eiswein, Beerenauslese, and Trockenbeerenauslese are luscious dessert wines. The Austrian system is similar, although the term "Kabinett" is not used, meaning dry Austrian Riesling has no designation of sweetness.

The New World has its own scale for Riesling. The International Riesling Foundation (IRF) has put together a scale based not only on sweetness levels but also acidity. The IRF rating can be found on the label of most New World Rieslings.

Riesling's popularity has made it popular in various regions of the world, but it ripens early. This means it can be quite overripe and bland in warm climates and it really does shine better in cooler climates. Besides Germany and Austria, the most recognized regions for noble Rieslings are Alsace; Clare Valley and Eden Valley in Australia; the Finger Lakes in New York; and Okanagan Valley in Canada.

Good with: Dry Riesling is easy to pair with many things such as citrus, rosemary, Thai food, fish, and lean meats. Sweeter styles of Riesling pair well with spicy Indian food and light, fruity desserts.

Try It with These Recipes: Fig, Camembert & Arugula Flatbreads (page 112); Chicken Wings with Spicy Maple Barbecue Sauce (page 118); Open-Faced Smoked Salmon Sandwiches (page 165); Shoyu-Style Ramen (page 180); Green Mango Salad with Peanut Sauce (page 151); Hoisin Chicken Lettuce Wraps (page 164); Chilled Zucchini Noodles with Coconut-Peanut Sauce (page 181); Ahi Tuna Tacos with Aioli (page 198)

Also Try: Muscat, Gewürztraminer, Pinot Gris, Torrontés

TORRONTÉS

Other Names: Torrontés Riojano, Torrontés Sanjuanino, Moscatel de Austria

Pronunciation: torr·ron·TEZ

Where It's Made: Argentina, Spain, Portugal

Recommended Producers: Alta Vista (Mendoza, Argentina), Susana Balbo (Mendoza, Argentina), Terrazas de los Andes (Mendoza, Argentina)

Overarching Characteristics: Aromatic, zesty, floral

Torrontés is the named shared among various similar varietals that can be found in Argentina, Spain, and Portugal. Torrontés Riojano is the most common, but there's also Torrontés Sanjuanino, Torrontés Mendocino, and many others. Because it thrives in high altitude, where it picks up vibrant acidity, Torrontés has become the emblematic white wine of Argentina, especially in high-elevation areas such as Cafayate in the Andes.

Torrontés is an aromatic, zesty, and floral varietal that's refreshing and light-bodied with intense acidity. When this grape is ripe enough, it can get a lovely exotic mandarin fruit and spicy expression. It's a truly interesting grape to try and it's very affordable.

Good with: Coconut, curries, poultry, fish, ceviches, empanadas

Try It with These Recipes: Garlic-Parmesan Roasted Edamame (page 104), Open-Faced Smoked Salmon Sandwiches (page 165), Green Mango Salad with Peanut Sauce (page 151), Chilled Zucchini Noodles with Coconut-Peanut Sauce (page 181)

Also Try: *Albariño, Riesling, Muscat*

MUSCAT

Other Names: Moscato, Moscatel, Muskat, Zibibbo, Muskotály

Pronunciation: muhs·KA

Where It's Made: Alsace, France, Italy, South Africa

Recommended Producers: Domaine Ostertag (Alsace, France), Navarro Vineyards (Anderson Valley, California), Chambers Rosewood Vineyards (Rutherglen, Australia),

Jean-Baptiste Arena (Cap Corse, France), Klein Constantia (South Africa), Telmo Rodríguez (Spain), Planeta (Sicily, Italy)

Overarching Characteristics: Aromatic, grapey, rose petal, perfumed

Muscat, like Pinot, is a big family of grape varietals. It's also one of the oldest, going back to Greek and Roman times. Muscat blancs à petits grains, also known as Muscat de Frontignan, is the most delicate and refined, and it's widespread all over the world. There's also Muscat of Alexandria, mostly found in Portugal, Spain, and South Africa. Muscat Ottonel is lighter and often used in blends. Generally low in acidity, but very expressive in terms of aromas and flavors, Muscat can be dry, sparkling, and even fortified, but it always keeps its very distinguishable grapey and floral character.

Italy is the biggest producer of Moscato, especially with its sparkling wines of Asti. Muscat can be found all over the world, but other notable regions include Muscat Beaumes de Venise, Clairette de Die, Vin de Constance, Rutherglen Muscat, Muscat du Cap Corse, Moscatel de Setúbal. In addition, it's part of the Alsatian Quatuor of noble grape varietals.

Good with: Dried fruits, hard cheeses, terrines, cheesecake, ice cream, creamy desserts

Try It with These Recipes: Key Lime Coconut Pie (page 132), Banana-Cinnamon Bread Pudding (page 123), Black Bean & Corn Chilaquiles (page 182)

Also Try: Pinot Gris, Gewürztraminer

GEWÜRZTRAMINER

Other Names: Klevner, Roter Traminer, Fromenteau

Pronunciation: geh·VAIRTZ·trah·mee·ner

Where It's Made: Alsace, California, Canada

Recommended Producers: Léon Beyer (Alsace, France), Domaine Barmès-Buecher (Alsace, France), Kolbenhof (Alto Adige, Italy), Cave Spring (Ontario, Canada), Dutton-Goldfield (Sonoma, California)

Overarching Characteristics: Aromatic, lychee, rose petal

Gewürztraminer grapes are tinted a grayish pink, and this pigment gives the wine its deep, golden color. This distinctive hue, combined with its very unique lychee and rose aromas, makes it one of the most easily recognizable wines. It's as aromatic as Moscato, but with more alcohol and a rounded texture. More complex and ripe expressions will also show some ginger, white pepper, and pineapple notes.

Many people think Gewürztraminer is always sweet, but the truth is, it only gives the impression of being sweet. The aromatic profile is so intense and fruity, you may confuse it for sweetness when, in fact, it's completely dry. This impression is enhanced by its lower acidity. The exceptions are Vendange Tardives and Sélection de Grains Nobles, which are, in fact, sweet.

Most Gewürztraminer comes from Alsace, where it shines, especially in Grand Cru appellations. There are interesting examples in North America, in the Niagara Peninsula in Canada, the Finger Lakes in New York, and in the cooler regions of California. Besides that, there are a few in Alto Adige in Italy and Australia, but in negligible quantities.

Good with: Tikka masala, samosas, chickpeas, kebab, ginger, sesame

Try It with These Recipes: Caramelized Onion Tart with Feta Cheese & Pine Nuts (page 111), Pork Dumplings with Spinach & Sesame (page 166), Chilled Zucchini Noodles with Coconut-Peanut Sauce (page 181), Ahi Tuna Tacos with Aioli (page 198)

Also Try: *Pinot Gris, Moscato, Grenache*

Rich & Bold Whites

RHÔNE WHITE BLENDS

Pronunciation: RONE

Where It's Made: Rhône Valley

Recommended Producers: Château Saint-Cosme (Gigondas, France), Château La Nerthe (Châteauneuf-du-Pape, France), E. Guigal (Condrieu, France), M. Chapoutier (Hermitage, France)

Overarching Characteristics: Medium-bodied, intense aromatic profile, medium to high alcohol, fruity, expressive

The South of France, including the Rhône Valley, is a champion at making blends. In Châteauneuf-du-Pape there are 18 different varieties allowed, and indeed, sometimes they may be all used in the same bottle. In most cases, the actual appellation is more telling than the grape used, unlike in the New World, where varietal labeling is the norm. Depending on the region, blends may differ depending on regulations, but they're usually Marsanne-dominant with varying addition of Roussanne, Viognier, Muscat, Grenache, Piquepoul, Clairette, Bourboulenc, Vermentino, and others.

The actual blend plays an important role in the final taste, but overall, Rhône white blends are a great medium-bodied options with a good intensity of flavors and varying aromatic profiles from fruity citrus and stone fruits to spice.

Similar blends are also found in Adelaide, Australia; California; and Catalonia.

Good with: Roast chicken, fried rice, stir-fries, oily fish

Try It with These Recipes: Gratin Dauphinois (page 170), Falafel with Tzatziki Sauce (page 156), Grilled Corn Chowder (page 179), Shellfish Paella (page 196)

Also Try: *Viognier, Languedoc-Roussillon whites, Xarel-lo, Catalunya whites*

CHARDONNAY

Other Names: Morillon, Pinot Chardonnay, Feiner Weisser Burgunder, Auxerrois

Pronunciation: shaar·duh·NEI

Where It's made: Worldwide

Recommended Producers: Domaine Laroche (Chablis, France) Catena Zapata (Mendoza, Argentina) Gundlach Bundschu (Sonoma, California), Louis Jadot (Burgundy, France), Maison Champy (Burgundy, France), Henschke (Barossa, Australia)

Overarching Characteristics: Neutral, crisp apple, tropical fruit

Chardonnay is the second-most-planted grape varietal in the world. The name had become such a marketing tool that a movement started against it in the 1990s called ABC, which stands for "Anything but Chardonnay." Chardonnay doesn't have a strong personality. It's hard to describe because it's offered in so many styles, from so many places, that it's tough to pin down. Basically, it's like a blank canvas for winemakers. It's susceptible to vinification methods and will have a strong aromatic complexity that results directly from these techniques: malolactic fermentation produces buttery Chardonnay; oak aging gives bold, oaky, rich Chardonnays; and so on. Climate also plays a role in the final product. Cooler climates will produce soft wines with aromas of crisp apples and citrus, whereas warmer climates will develop stone fruit, bananas, guava, pineapple, and melon flavors.

OAKED CHARDONNAY

Rich, creamy examples of Chardonnay are found in Burgundy and California. These are the most complex examples with bold expression, heavy body, and an overall powerful style.

UNOAKED CHARDONNAY

Unoaked Chardonnays are delicate, lean, and mineral-driven. Chablis is the epitome of crisp Chardonnay wine. Other regions recognized for unoaked Chardonnay include Carneros in California, Tasmania in Australia, New Zealand, and Argentina.

Overall, Chardonnay is one of the most acclaimed wine varieties for its elegance and potential. Some bottles can even get to quite the extreme price range, and there's a Chardonnay for every occasion. Some of the most famous wines in the world are Chardonnays such as Montrachet, Meursault, and Corton-Charlemagne, but it can also be your everyday drink.

Good with: Unoaked Chardonnay goes with seafood, sushi, oysters, delicate fish, and risotto. Oaked Chardonnay can pair with heavier meals like pork chops with apples, roasted vegetables, and creamy pastas.

Try It with These Recipes: Eggs Benedict with Avocado (page 144), Creamy Cole-slaw with Jicama (page 150), Classic Lobster Bisque (page 160), Tempura Shrimp (page 162), Falafel with Tzatziki Sauce (page 156), Broiled Oysters with Gremolata (page 163), Grilled Corn Chowder (page 179), Gnocchi with Shiitake-Mozzarella Sauce (page 193), Coconut-Curry Halibut en Papillote (page 202)

Also Try: *Viognier, Roussane, Marsanne*

VIOGNIER

Pronunciation: vee·oh·NYEI

Where It's Made: Rhône Valley

Recommended Producers: Georges Vernay (Condrieu, France), E. Guigal (Condrieu, France), François Villard (Condrieu, France), Yves Cuilleron (Condrieu, France)

Overarching Characteristics: Apricot, blossom, heavy-bodied, golden

Viognier was so unpopular at some point in the mid-1980s that it almost completely disappeared. It is an intense grape varietal that is hard to grow, and hard to make right. Alcohol levels tend to be high, and it's not a very productive grape. However, when done properly, you get a unique and spectacular result.

The home of Viognier is in Northern Rhône, in the subregion of Condrieu, where it is the exclusive varietal grown. It is there on the very steep terraces, blown by the strong regional wind called Mistral, that we can find the best expressions combining body, texture, and intense aromatic profiles. Viognier is very aromatic with aromas of apricot, honeysuckle, beeswax, peach, and perfume. It's heavy on the palate with creamy body, low acidity, and textural weight.

Outside of Condrieu, Viognier has found a place in many Southern French blends, often joined by Roussane, Marsanne, Bourboulenc, White Grenache, and Vermentino. It's a good ingredient to add volume and flavor.

Good with: Roasted meats, chicken, pork, creamy cheeses, fondue, strong flavors such as saffron

Try It with These Recipes: Creamy Carrot & Ginger Soup (page 153), Crab Cakes with Tangerine Salsa (page 158), Gnocchi with Shiitake-Mozzarella Sauce (page 193), Shellfish Paella (page 196)

Also Try: *Moscatel, Trebbiano, Müller Thurgau, Roussane, Marsanne*

Rosé Wines

PROVENCE ROSÉ

Pronunciation: pro-VAHNS

Where It's Made: South of France

Recommended Producers: Domaine Ott (Côtes de Provence, France), Domaine de la Bégude (Bandol, France), Domaine des Béates (Coteaux d'Aix-en-Provence, France), Château Vignelaure (Coteaux d'Aix-en-Provence, France)

Overarching Characteristics: Fresh, high acidity, light, pale-colored, floral, grapefruit, delicate berries, mineral

More than a craze, rosé has become a lifestyle. Closely linked to summer and sipping poolside, the perception of rosé is borderline frivolous, when in fact they are quite serious wines. Provence, although small, produces a quarter of all the worldwide rosé production. Aside from a few exceptions, most Provence wines are usually a blend of Grenache, Mourvèdre, Cinsault, Syrah, and Counoise. Cabernet Sauvignon and other grapes are also grown in the region. Depending on the appellation, styles and varietals vary.

Côte de Provence is the largest of these appellations, and their rosés are tight and bright, with delicate aromas of grapefruit, melon, and violet. The Coteaux d'Aix en Provence growing area is windier, which gives aromatic depth and a fruit-forward character, with notes of white peach and red berries. Coteaux Varois de Provence, the heart of the province, has soils mainly composed of limestone, which, combined with the high altitude, produce wines with good acidity and complex aromas and structure. Bandol, although very small area, is quite unique. It produces Mourvèdre-based rosés with a lot of structure and wild-game aromas. It feels as if the Provençal cuisine was made especially for rosé: A Niçoise salad with a fresh Côte de Provence or a classic bouillabaisse with Bandol are iconic matches.

Good with: Salads, vegetables, eggs, salmon, goat cheeses, grapefruits, melon

Try It with These Recipes: Beet Carpaccio & Goat Cheese with Pink Grapefruit Dressing (page 108), Heirloom Tomato & Peach Bruschetta (page 110), Grilled Fruit

Caprese Salad (page 149), Tempura Shrimp (page 162), Summer Gazpacho with Asiago-Garlic Toast (page 152), Ahi Tuna Tacos with Aioli (page 198)

Also Try: *Tavel, Bandol, Rosé des Riceys, Sancerre Rosé, Marsannay Rosé*

OTHER ROSÉ WINES

Where It's Made: Worldwide

Recommended Producers: Gérard Bertrand (Languedoc-Roussillon), Château d'Aqueria (Tavel), Barone di Villagrande (Etna) Marchesi de Frescobaldi (Tuscany), Bodega Villa d'Orta (Spain)

Overarching Characteristics: Fresh, high acidity, colorful, floral, grapefruit, delicate berries

Provence may be the leader in rosé, but it's definitely not the only place to find these fancy pink delights. Here are a few places to look for other styles of rosé:

OTHER FRENCH ROSÉS

Tavel: In the Rhône Valley, Tavel primarily uses Grenache. They produce dry rosés with deep, vibrant pink colors and red fruit aromas. They have more structure, and even some tannins.

Corsica: Light and elegant, with similar maritime influences to Provence, these rosés use fun local grapes in blends such as Nielluccio and Sciacarello.

Loire Valley: Cabernet Franc and Pinot Noir as well as Grolleau makes rosés with strong character in the Loire Valley. Look for Rosé d'Anjou, Chinon for spicy rosé, or Sancerre Rosé.

Spanish Rosado: Spanish Rosados are quite different from French Rosés. They're fruitier and darker in color, with dense structure. Tempranillo and Grenache are the most used grape varietals. Navarre is the most recognized region for rosé, but you can find some all over Spain, including Rioja.

ITALIAN ROSATO

Depending on where you are in Italy, the style will be quite distinct. Rosés from Northern Italy are light and fruity with fresh and elegant styles. You'll find them in

Veneto, Friuli-Venezia Giulia, Trentino-Alto Adige, and Chiaretto in Lombardy.

Cerasuolo d'Abruzzo, an appellation in Central Italy, is dedicated to bright pink, simple, fruity rosé.

The south of Italy, with its warmer climate, has bolder, more intense rosés with lots of flavors and structure. Look for Nero d'Avola–based rosé in Sicily, or Negroamaro-based rosé in Puglia.

Everywhere there's wine, there can be rosé. New Zealand Pinot Noir Rosé, Austrian Blaufränkisch Rosé, the multitude of Californian examples such as Cabernet-based rosés, and Greece's Agiorgitiko Rosé are just a few examples worth seeking out.

Good with: Shrimp, paté, charcuterie, chorizo, tapenade, olives, aioli, grilled fish, tomatoes, feta, melon, beets

Try It with These Recipes: Beet Carpaccio & Goat Cheese with Pink Grapefruit Dressing (page 108), Heirloom Tomato & Peach Bruschetta (page 110), Grilled Fruit Caprese Salad (page 149), Tempura Shrimp (page 162), Summer Gazpacho with Asiago-Garlic Toast (page 152), Crunchy Chopped Vegetable Tabbouleh (page 174), Pizza Margherita (page 184)

Also Try: *Marsannay Rosé, Bordeaux Rosé, Cava Rosé, Champagne Rosé*

Chapter 4

Red Wines

DELICATE REDS

FRIENDLY, MODERATE REDS

POWERFUL REDS

Know Your Red Wine

With varieties of red wine grapes numbering in the hundreds, there is as much to learn about red wine as there are grapes on a vine. Don't worry, you don't need to know everything about them to be able to enjoy a glass.

There are two things to know about what makes red wine unique. One is the color. Most red grapes have clear flesh. The color comes from the skins that have been macerated, soaked, and mixed with the juice. The shade of your red wine can actually tell you a lot. If the color is pale, you're probably looking at a light style of wine. If your wine is dark and opaque, get your palate ready—it's going to be potent. The color alone offers hints on how to do your pair. It's actually rather intuitive.

Second, when considering how to pair red wines, there's a characteristic that you can't overlook: tannins. It's an important part of the palate of red wine. Tannins are not a flavor, but a sensation. They are responsible for the drying, astringent effect wine has on your mouth. Tannins are not exclusive to wine: The compound, called polyphenols, can also be found in wood, seeds, and fruit skins. In the case of grapes, polyphenols, which are naturally present in the skins, stems, and seeds, are released into the juice when macerated.

Though some grapes have more polyphenols than others, other factors can also impact the level of tannins. Intense maceration time, which means more contact between the juice and the skins and pips (seeds), can make wines more tannic. There are tannins in oak, which means that a wine with extended maturation in oak barrels will have extra tannic structure. Tannins do more than make your mouth pucker. They act as an antioxidant, which makes tannic wines age-worthy. They love fat and rich foods. Polyphenols interact with proteins by binding to them, which means that taking a sip of a big Cabernet Sauvignon after a bite of a porterhouse steak, for instance, changes the mouthfeel of the wine from dry and grippy to smooth and less astringent.

A bold statement like "red wine always goes with meat" just isn't accurate. There's a world of differences between a light red and a heavy red. Getting to know the characteristics of individual wines will help you better understand the nuances of their qualities, and the foods that they go with best.

A WORD ABOUT RED WINE BLENDS

What's in a blend? Imagine having an unlimited palette of colors to create a masterpiece. Winemaking is, in so many ways, similar to making art. The winemaker's choices through-out the process are the creative touches that make each wine unique.

They can either go with a monochrome look, with a single-varietal or single-vineyard, or they can play around and get the best of every grape available to them. Most wines are blended to some extent. In the United States, a bottle that's labeled as being a certain varietal needs at least 75 percent of that grape. So, if you pick up a Merlot wine, there may be up to 25 percent that's up to the winemaker's discretion.

Each grape varietal has its own attributes. Some add color, like Petit Verdot or Syrah; some add fruitiness, like Grenache; some will soften a blend, like Cinsault; whereas some will add flavor and complexity. Some blends are famous. Bordeaux blends are typically a mix of Cabernet Sauvignon, Merlot, Cabernet Franc, Malbec, and Petit Verdot, but it was so popular that the term was exported. Historically, vineyards used to be **complanted**, with various varieties all mixed. Now, in most cases, the wines from different grapes will be vinified separately, and then blended afterward. It's just about having options.

Delicate Reds

GAMAY

Other Names: Gamay Noir à Jus Blanc

Pronunciation: gam·MEH

Where It's Made: Beaujolais

Recommended Producers: Jean-Paul Brun (Beaujolais), Jean Foillard (Morgon, Beaujolais), Marcel Lapierre (Morgon, Beaujolais), Jean-Paul Thévenet (Morgon, Beaujolais), Domaine du Moulin-à-Vent (Moulin-à-Vent, Beaujolais)

Overarching Characteristics: Light-bodied, fruit-driven, candy

Grown predominantly in Beaujolais, Gamay is as delicate as it can get in terms of red wine. It has predominant aromas of cherries and strawberries, but can also have candied fruit notes. Beaujolais is known for using **carbonic maceration**, a vinification method that consists of fermenting whole-cluster berries in an oxygen-free environment. The berries start to ferment from the inside and can give off a bubble-gum character. This technique is mostly used for Beaujolais nouveau: young wines released the third Thursday of November, right after the harvest. These wines are a tradition, but they don't express the complete potential of the grape and the terroir.

If you want the best expressions of Gamay, you need to look for the 10 Crus of Beaujolais: Saint-Amour, Morgon, Moulin-à-Vent, Chiroubles, Regnié, Brouilly, Côte de Brouilly, Chénas, Fleurie, and Juliénas. The wines from these villages are usually vinified traditionally and are aged in oak.

Outside of Beaujolais, Gamay is also used in blends, usually with Pinot Noir. It's planted in Switzerland, in the Dôle department, and can also be found in some specific appellation of France like Passe-Tout-Grains in Burgundy or Saint-Pourçain in Loire.

Good with: Charcuterie, ham, roast chicken, cranberry sauce

Try It with These Recipes: Shoyu-Style Ramen (page 180), Falafel with Tzatziki Sauce (page 156), Roasted Root Vegetable Borscht (page 178)

Also Try: Pinot Noir, Zweigelt, Blaufränkisch, Bourgogne Passe-Tout-Grains

MENCÍA

Other Names: Jaén

Pronunciation: men·SEE·ah

Where It's Made: Northwest Spain

Recommended Producers: Descendientes de J. Palacios (Bierzo, Spain), Dominio de Tares (Bierzo, Spain), Pittacum (Bierzo, Spain), Losada (Bierzo, Spain), Raúl Pérez (Bierzo, Spain)

Overarching Characteristics: Fresh acidity, fine tannins, black fruits, herbs, root vegetables, onions, olives

Pale, light, and fragrant, Mencía has only recently gained popularity internationally. Predominantly found in the region of Bierzo in the Spanish province of León, near Galicia, it was quite unknown until the 1990s. That's when a handful of ambitious producers saw potential in the old abandoned vineyards and set out to revive them. Most of the Mencía plantings in Bierzo are from vines that are at least half a century old. Old vines are treasured because they bring extra concentration, texture, and flavor to wines. Bierzo is experiencing a rebirth and it's all thanks to the refined wines from old bush vines of Mencía.

Mencía wines have vibrant acidity but also a rich texture. Together, the freshness and volume give a nice balance as well as versatility. The aromas can be quite complex with red and black fruits, leather, dried herbs, oak, and licorice.

Good with: Rosemary, Moroccan food, grilled fish, octopus, couscous, beans and lentils, grilled vegetables

Try It with These Recipes: Shoyu-Style Ramen (page 180), Falafel with Tzatziki Sauce (page 156), Black Bean & Corn Chilaquiles (page 182), Ahi Tuna Tacos with Aioli (page 198), Smoked Meat Sandwiches with Grilled Vegetables (page 212)

Also Try: Pinot Noir, Gamay, Grenache

PINOT NOIR

Other Names: Spätburgunder, Blauburgunder, Pinot Nero

Pronunciation: PEE·no n·WAR

Where It's Made: Worldwide

Recommended Producers: Bouchard Père et Fils (Bourgogne, France), Domaine Leroy (Bourgogne, France), Faiveley (Bourgogne, France), Etude (Oregon, United States), Domaine Serene (Oregon, United States), Résonance (Oregon, United States), Two Paddock (Central Otago, New Zealand)

Overarching Characteristics: Elegant and charming, light-bodied, red cherries, mushroom, clove

The star grape of Burgundy, Pinot Noir is the most popular of the light grape varietals. It is a high-class grape and makes some of the most iconic and renowned wines in the world, like Domaine de la Romanée-Conti and La Tâche.

Pinot Noir is now found internationally, but regions beside Burgundy are also famous for it: Oregon, cooler regions of California such as Carneros and the Russian River Valley, Alsace, Jura, Sancerre, Germany (under the name Spätburgunder), Austria (under the name Blauburgunder), Australia's Yarra Valley and Tasmania, and New Zealand. It would probably be the most planted varietal if it weren't so hard to grow. It is susceptible to frost and rot, and the berries are delicate, thin-skinned, and ripen early, which means it's not suitable for warm climates.

Pinot Noir is called grape of the thousand clones. A vine **clone** is when you take a cutting from a selected "Mother Vine" and plant it or graft it to a rootstock. It is used to genetically maintain characteristics in vines (such as resistance to disease, quality, and flavors). They're the same grape but with slight variations. In fact, there are more than 40 different clones of Pinot Noir with different quality levels and attributes.

Good with: Oily fish, aged beef, duck, salmon, grilled tuna, mushrooms, lamb

Try It with These Recipes: Wild Mushroom Arancini (page 116), Classic Canadian Poutine (page 122), Hoisin Chicken Lettuce Wraps (page 164), Roasted Root Vegetable Borscht (page 178), Ahi Tuna Tacos with Aioli (page 198), Cornish Hens with Figs & Walnuts (page 204)

Also Try: *Gamay, Mencía, Poulsard*

POULSARD

Other Names: Ploussard

Pronunciation: pool·SAHR

Where It's Made: Jura, France

Recommended Producers: Domaine Tissot (Arbois, France), Domaine Rijckaert (Arbois, France), Domaine Rolet (Arbois, France)

Overarching Characteristics: Light-colored, lightweight, savory aromas, mushroom, wild berries

Poulsard is the specialty of Arbois in the Jura, near the Swiss border. These red wine grapes have very thin skins and a very pale garnet color, which is so pale that some examples appear closer to rosé. The character of the wine is also light and perfumed with stunning, delicate aromas of mushrooms, wild strawberries, and an overall savory style. It has vibrant acidity and offers fantastic versatility when it comes to food pairing. Try it with Comté and Morbier, two cheeses produced in the Jura region that are natural mates for its wines.

Poulsard is a rarity, as it's only produced in one of the smallest regions of France. However, it is hard to leave out since it's such a food-friendly wine. It is an original and refined choice.

Good with Mushrooms, cream sauces, nutty cheeses, charcuterie, poultry, ham, cheesy foods

Try It with These Recipes: Wild Mushroom Arancini (page 116), Gratin Dauphinois (page 170), Gnocchi with Shiitake-Mozzarella Sauce (page 193)

Also Try: *Pinot Noir, Gamay, Trousseau*

BLAUFRÄNKISCH

Other Names: Lemberger, Kékfrankos

Pronunciation: blo·frann·KEESH

Where It's Made: Austria, New York

Recommended Producers: Schiefer (Burgenland, Austria), Prieler (Burgenland, Austria), Dr. Frank Konstantin (Finger Lakes, New York)

Overarching Characteristics: Perfumed, pomegranate, black cherries, smooth

Originally from Austria, Blaufränkisch is also known as Lemberger in Germany and Kéfrankos in Hungary. Its name is not exactly the easiest to pronounce, and this is why recent plantings and experiments in North America (New York, Washington, and British Columbia) tend to use the German name, Lemberger. By any name, it's a great, friendly option to accompany your meals because of its freshness, fruitiness, and soft tannins.

A typical Blaufränkisch is characterized by black fruits, cherries, pomegranate, and a smoky, peppery flavor. It's quite elegant with strong acidity, but also distinctive velvety tannins.

Good with: Wild game, duck, poultry, smoked sausage, tomato-based sauces, chili, smoked Gouda, sweet potatoes

Try It with These Recipes: Classic Lobster Bisque (page 160), Lamb Sliders with Brie (page 171), Ahi Tuna Tacos with Aioli (page 198)

Also Try: Mencía, St. Laurent

Friendly, Moderate Reds

GRENACHE

Other Names: Garnacha, Garnatxa, Cannonau, Lladoner, Alicante, Tinta de Aragón

Pronunciation: greh·NASH or ghar·NHA·tcha

Where It's Made: Spain, South of France

Recommended Producers: Château de Beaucastel (Châteauneuf-du-Pape, France), Torbreck Vintners (Barossa, Australia), Alvaro Palacios (Priorat, Spain), Alto Moncayo (Campo de Borja, Spain), Domaine Cazes (Roussillon, France)

Overarching Characteristics: Fresh, juicy, red fruit aromas, olives, soft palate

Grenache is the seventh most widely planted grape in the world. It's a key component in many blends like the celebrated wines of Châteauneuf-du-Pape or Priorat, but Grenache is also featured in single-variety wines. More often than not, it acts as a silent hero. It has a supporting role in blends by providing bright berry flavors and freshness. It's also part of the classic Côtes du Rhône blend, commonly called GSM, which stands for Grenache, Syrah, and Mourvèdre.

Grenache is adaptable and versatile. It was born in the Spanish region of Aragón, and has proven to be quite the resilient variety. It manages to survive in inhospitable regions while resisting unfavorable weather conditions and a host of diseases. This is why you can find some precious century-old vines. These valuable ancient vines are part of the history of a place, but they are also to be treasured for their concentrated flavors, well-established roots, and overall terroir and quality-driven expressions. Whereas most Grenache tends to be light and simple, old vine Grenache has added complexity, rich texture, and depth.

Depending on where it comes from, Grenache can have different expressions. Although it can be very fruity and light on its own or in some Southern French blends, a powerful Gigondas or Campo de Borja will be at the complete opposite of the strength spectrum. Regardless, Grenache is a source of freshness and acidity, which is always welcome with food.

It can be found in many regions of Spain, the Rhône Valley, Languedoc-Roussillon, Provence, and in Sardinia under the name Cannonau. Old vines of Grenache are also being preserved in Australia and South Africa.

Good with: Herbs, roasted meats, rabbit, chicken, pork, tapenade

Try It with These Recipes: Pomegranate-Glazed Turkey Meatballs (page 120), Hoisin Chicken Lettuce Wraps (page 164), Black Bean & Corn Chilaquiles (page 182)

Also Try: Cinsault, Côtes du Rhône, Châteauneuf-du-Pape, Côtes-du-Roussillon

BARBERA

Other Names: Barbera d'Alba, Barbera d'Aosta, Barbera Sarda, Barbera d'Asti, Barbera del Monferrato

Pronunciation: bar·BEH·rah

Where It's Made: Piedmont, Italy

Recommended Producers: Michele Chiarlo (Piedmont, Italy), Braida di Giacomo (Piedmont, Italy), Fontanafredda (Piedmont, Italy), Vietti (Piedmont, Italy)

Overarching Characteristics: Dark black color; light, juicy taste; red berries; violet; anise

Italian to the core, Barbera is like Nebbiolo's little brother. It's grown in Piedmont, like the prized Nebbiolo, and is the region's most widely planted varietal. Barbera is a fun red, and an easy-to-like, quite affordable, day-to-day wine. It's the kind of bottle you'd want to open with a simple plate of pasta or take-out pizza. It's attractive with a beautiful dark color, but a light, juicy taste with aromas of dried red berries, violet, anis, and food-friendly high acids.

Following Italian tradition, Barbera takes on the name of the places it grows on labels. Some appellations are dedicated to this varietal: Barbera d'Alba, Barbera d'Aosta, Barbera Sarda, Barbera d'Asti, Barbera del Monferrato, and the most recently recognized (2016) Nizza designation. California, with its tendency to like Italian varietals, also has some examples of Barbera that are a little bit bolder, with spices and more concentration.

Good with: Herbs, root vegetables, rich meats, cherry, sage, fennel, tajarin, porcini mushrooms, pizza

Try It with These Recipes: Creamy Carrot & Ginger Soup (page 153); Classic Lobster Bisque (page 160); Cheesy Cherry-Tomato Bread Pudding (page 145); Beet Ravioli with Ricotta Cheese, Orange, Pistachio & Parsley (page 186); Smoked Meat Sandwiches with Grilled Vegetables (page 212)

Also Try: Dolcetto, Langhe Nebbiolo, Chianti

CARIGNAN

Other Names: Cariñena, Carignane, Carignano, Mazuelo, Gragnano, Pinot Evara, Samsó

Pronunciation: cah·REE·nyan

Where It's Made: Spain, Languedoc-Roussillon

Recommended Producers: Terroir al Límit (Priorat, Spain), Vall Llach (Priorat, Spain), Domaine de l'Aupilhac (Languedoc-Roussillon, France), Domaine Léon Barral (Languedoc-Roussillon, France)

Overarching Characteristics: Cranberries, baking spices, earth, concentrated, rich

Most wine drinkers have never even heard of Carignan. It's originally from Spain in the similarly named region Cariñena, in Aragón, but it became closely linked with Catalonia. The old bush vines of Carignan in Priorat are especially treasured for their concentrated flavors.

In the 20th century, Carignan was more planted in Spain and France than Merlot. It can be extremely fruitful, and was planted for bulk production of wine. When a shift toward quality became more fashionable in these producing regions, Carignan was cast aside. It's by rediscovering old vineyards that producers started to understand its capacity to produce surprisingly rich, fruit-driven, flavorful wines. It has a good concentration and intensity of flavors, ripe fruit character, earthiness, baking spices, and supple tannins.

Although single-varietal Carignan from old vines are becoming more popular, this varietal is still mostly used as a blending partner to Grenache in Languedoc-Roussillon and Catalonia. It brings a good backbone to a blend, with body and color.

Good with: Roast meats, duck, root vegetables, spices, cranberry sauce, brisket

Try It with These Recipes: Falafel with Tzatziki Sauce (page 156); Beet Ravioli with Ricotta Cheese, Orange, Pistachio & Parsley (page 186)

Also Try: *Cinsault, Grenache, Syrah*

RHÔNE VALLEY BLENDS AND GSM BLENDS

Pronunciation: RONE

Where It's Made: Rhône Valley

Recommended Producers: Château de Saint-Cosme (Gigondas, Rhône Valley), Tardieu-Laurent (Luberon, Rhône Valley), Château de Beaucastel (Châteauneuf-du-Pape, Rhône Valley)

Overarching Characteristics: Fruit-forward, rounded, ripe, **garrigue** (scrub-land aroma)

Grenache, Syrah, and Mourvèdre make up an iconic trio in the wine world. The indigenous grapes found in the Rhône Valley and Côtes du Rhône appellation can stand alone, but the sum is greater than its parts. Grenache brings fruitiness and a smooth palate, Syrah brings structure and spiciness, and Mourvèdre completes the complexity with a unique earthy and gamey flavor profile. It's a perfect partnership.

The Rhône Valley blend can include even more grape varieties, but the concept is the same: to use the force and abilities of each grape to build up a balanced and complex wine.

In the 1980s, a group of Californian winemakers decided to promote Rhône varieties—which weren't exactly popular in California, where Cabernet Sauvignon and Merlot are kings. Bonny Doon Vineyard, Qupé, and Tablas Creek, in the central coast of California, started the Rhône Rangers, an association that has since grown to 100 wineries. For example, Ridge Vineyards, which produces some of the most sought-after wines in the region, uses Rhône varietals in their blends.

Good with: Pizza, ham, ratatouille, grilled tuna

Try It with These Recipes: Crispy Shrimp with Romesco Sauce (page 114), Lamb Sliders with Brie (page 171), Roasted Vegetable Chili with Crème Fraîche (page 188), Grilled Sirloin with Herb & Blue Cheese Compound Butter (page 203)

Also Try: Languedoc-Roussillon, Grenache, Côtes du Rhône

SANGIOVESE

Other Names: Brunello, Vino Nobile, Prugnolo, Morellino, Nielluccio, Sanvicetro, Sangioveto

Pronunciation: san·jeeoh·VAY·zeh

Where It's Made: Tuscany, Italy

Recommended Producers: Isole e Olena (Chianti Classico, Italy), Caparzo (Brunello di Montalcino, Italy), Fattoria dei Barbi (Brunello di Montalcino, Italy), Carpineto (Vino Nobile di Montepulciano, Italy)

Overarching Characteristics: Cherries, black tea, aromatic, high acidity, balanced tannins

All the main red wine appellations of Tuscany use Sangiovese. It's high in tannins, high in mouthwatering acidity, and short on color, with a fresh, fruity and savory aromatic profile. However, it can be confusing, as Sangiovese has many different names and clones, some with distinctive expressions.

BRUNELLO DI MONTALCINO: Brunello is a Sangiovese clone that is darker in color with more structure and body. It's made in the village of Montalcino and must be aged for at least four years. If the term Riserva is used, the aging requirement is five years.

CHIANTI CLASSICO: Chianti Classico is a specific, historical region within the larger Chianti appellation. Wines must be at least 80 percent Sangiovese. In terms of style, Chianti and Chianti Classico should not be mixed up. Chianti tends to be lighter and simpler, whereas Chianti Classico has longer aging requirements and a bolder, balanced style.

SUPER TUSCANS: These are wines made under the Toscana **IGT (Indicazione Geografica Tipica**), to allow more freedom to producers. These are blends of

Sangiovese grapes with international varieties (Merlot, Cabernet Sauvignon, Cabernet Franc).

VINO NOBILE DI MONTEPULCIANO: This type of wine is also a Sangiovese-based blend, referred to locally using the synonym Vino Nobile, made near the village of Montepulciano. It's not to be confused with Montepulciano d'Abruzzo, which is a wine from the Montepulciano grape variety made in Abruzzo.

ROSSO: Rosso is a term used to designate a simpler, young style of Sangiovese. Rosso di Montalcino, Rosso di Montepulciano, and Toscana Rosso are all Sangiovese-based.

Good with: Tomato-based sauces, smoked meat, osso bucco, braised beef, bistecca fiorentina

Try It with These Recipes: Pomegranate-Glazed Turkey Meatballs (page 120), Cheesy Cherry-Tomato Bread Pudding (page 145), Pizza Margherita (page 184), Chicken Cacciatore (page 206)

Also Try: Brunello di Montalcino, Chianti Classico, Vino Nobile di Montepulciano, Maremma

CABERNET FRANC

Other Names: Bordo, Bouchet, Bouchy, Breton

Pronunciation: ca·bear·NAY FRAHN

Where It's Made: Bordeaux and Loire Valley

Recommended Producers: Yannick Amirault (Bourgueil, Loire Valley), Philippe Alliet (Chinon, Loire Valley), Domaine des Roches Neuves (Saumur-Champigny, Loire Valley), Le Macchiole (Tuscany, Italy), Clos des Jacobins (Saint-Émilion, Bordeaux), Château Chauvin (Saint-Émilion, Bordeaux), Lamoreaux Landing (Finger Lakes, New York)

Overarching Characteristics: Roasted red pepper, jalapeño pepper, green bell pepper, tannic

Cabernet Franc is often described as the softer counterpart to Cabernet Sauvignon. The latter is bold and powerful, whereas Cabernet Franc is rather gentle.

In fact, Cabernet Franc and Sauvignon Blanc are the parent varietals that created Cabernet Sauvignon.

It's a robust grape that can thrive in various climates and locations. Typical expressions will have aromas of red or green bell pepper, plum, and black fruits as well as forest floor and gravel. Light in color and flirty, it also has a structured palate with bold tannins, high acidity, and intensity. The earthiness of Cabernet Franc makes it a great match to wild game such as boar and rabbit, and all sorts of patés and rillettes.

Cabernet Franc is an important part of Bordeaux blends, especially as a partner to Merlot in parts of Saint-Émilion. It can also be found in Chinon, Bourgueuil, and Saumur-Champigny appellations in the Loire Valley. After France, Italy is the second biggest producer of Cabernet Franc. It's mostly used in blends with other international varieties. In California, it's found in many red blends, but its main home is in the Sierra Foothills. Basically, everywhere you can find Bordeaux blends (Australia, Chile, etc.), you can find Cabernet Franc.

Good with: Grilled vegetables, beans, barbecue sauce, tomato-based dishes

Try It with These Recipes: Beet Carpaccio & Goat Cheese with Pink Grapefruit Dressing (page 108), Crispy Shrimp with Romesco Sauce (page 114), Eggplant Paprikash (page 192)

Also Try: Saint-Émilion, Merlot, Carignan

MERLOT

Other Names: Petit Merle

Pronunciation: murr·LOW

Where It's Made: Worldwide

Recommended Producers: Château la Croix Labrie (Saint Émilion, Bordeaux), Château Trotanoy (Pomerol, Bordeaux), Tenuta dell'Ornellaia (Tuscany, italy), Tenuta Argentiera (Tuscany, Italy), Duckhorn (Napa Valley, California)

Overarching Characteristics: Plum, cocoa, affinity to oak, velvety tannins

Merlot is the most planted red grape varietal in the world. It can easily adapt to various climates, even cooler areas where Cabernet Sauvignon struggles to grow. It has moderate acidity and alcohol, and it's recognized for its plump plum aromas, chocolate notes, and affinity to oak ("affinity to oak" means the wine will easily showcase oak aromas such as clove, vanilla, and cedar). Merlot can be hard to recognize, especially since it's often used in blends with Cabernet Sauvignon, but its velvety tannins are an easy tell. It's this smoother character that makes it ideal with leaner meats like lamb, chicken, or even a meat lasagna.

Merlot has made the rounds. It is the predominant grape variety on the right bank of the Garonne River in Bordeaux, and in Saint-Émilion and Pomerol. It is widespread throughout the rest of France, often in a blend, partnered with Malbec and Syrah. Merlot is the fourth-most-planted varietal in the United States, with some of the biggest, boldest expressions coming from California and Washington. In Italy, it joined Cabernet Sauvignon and Sangiovese in the super Tuscan trend, and makes an appearance in the iconic Sassicaia wine from the Tuscan region of Bolgheri. Merlot is also an important varietal in Chile.

Good with: Chicken, turkey, pork, burgers, stews

Try It with These Recipes: Mediterranean-Inspired Pasta Frittata (page 146), Eggplant Paprikash (page 192), Chicken Cacciatore (page 206), Braised Lamb Shanks with Rosemary & Red Wine Sauce (page 214)

Also Try: *Cabernet Franc, Zinfandel, Malbec*

ZINFANDEL

Other Names: Primitivo, Crljenak Kaštelanski

Pronunciation: ZIN·fahn·del

Where It's Made: California, Puglia, Croatia

Recommended Producers: Turley Wine Cellars (California), Seghesio (Sonoma, California), Ridge Vineyards (California), Tormaresca (Puglia, Italy)

Overarching Characteristics: Jammy, blackberries, raisin, cinnamon, vanilla, high alcohol, sweetness

Zinfandel originated in Croatia under the name Crljenak Kaštelanski, which means "red grapes of Kaštela," the town where it was found. However, over the years,

California became its spiritual home. It was first grown in the United States in the 1820s by George Gibbs, a plant nursery owner on Long Island, who brought cuttings from the Imperial Collection of Plant Species in Vienna. The grape spread quickly, and was soon embraced by California growers. By 1888, a third of all the grapevines in the United States were Zinfandel. Even at this stage in California's young wine-making history, Zinfandel can safely be called the flagship grape.

Zinfandel is a curious varietal. Its main issue is that it struggles to ripen evenly. This means you'll get bunches of thick skin grapes with some berries that are still green, some at peak maturity and some that are shriveled and **raisinated**. This is why it can be either very light on the palate or quite concentrated, depending on the overall maturity. It's not exactly a powerful red as it doesn't have much tannins, but what it lacks in tannins it makes up for in alcohol content and sweetness. Some examples of Zinfandels can reach up to 17 to 18 percent ABV, which is the maximum level in which yeasts can survive. This alcohol level and weight can be tricky during pairing, but the sweetness of Zinfandel gives it some versatility, too. Always check the alcohol level of your bottle before trying to pair it. If it's higher than 15 percent, avoid spiciness, but definitely try it with heavy braised meat and briskets.

In Puglia, Italy, Zinfandel is known under the name Primitivo. Italian expressions are also quite concentrated, with jammy fruits and a rustic character.

Good with: Dark chocolate, curry, spices, cinnamon, vanilla, barbecue

Try It with These Recipes: Chicken Wings with Spicy Maple Barbecue Sauce (page 118), Mediterranean-Inspired Pasta Frittata (page 146), Molasses Baked Beans with Salt Pork (page 168)

Also Try: Negroamaro, Merlot, Amarone

VALPOLICELLA BLENDS

Pronunciation: val·po·lee·CHE·lah

Where It's Made: Veneto, Italy

Recommended Producers: Tenuta Sant'Antonio (Valpolicella, Italy), Tedeschi (Valpolicella, Italy), Speri (Valpolicella, Italy), Masi (Valpolicella, Italy)

Overarching Characteristics: Rich, concentrated, cherries, dried fruits, sweetness

Valpolicella is one of the biggest producing appellations in terms of volume—its name translates directly to "valley of many cellars." This fertile region also has a very unique way of producing wines. The blends are always similar, and only indigenous grape varieties are allowed: mostly Corvina, Corvinone, Rondinella, Molinara, and Oseleta, but there are actually four different styles.

Valpolicella Classico: Valpolicella Classico makes up a vast majority of the production. They're the lighter-styled, fresh, and fruity expression of the region. It's easy drinking and quite simple.

Amarone della Valpolicella: Amarone wines are made with dried grapes, which are called Passito. The slightly raisinated grapes completely change the profile. It gets rich and concentrated, with a bit of sweetness and lovely aromas of cherries, cocoa, and dried fruits.

Valpolicella Ripasso: Ripasso means re-pass. When Amarone is done, producers can hold on to the grape skins and add it to newly made Valpolicella wines. This creates an in-between style. It's more complex than Valpolicella Classico, but not as concentrated and raisinated as Amarone.

Recioto della Valpolicella: Similarily to Amarone, Recioto is also made from dried grapes, but instead of being dry to off-dry, it's fully sweet. It's a tradition in the region and was produced way before Amarone.

Good with: Risotto, braised beef, strong cheeses, game meats, chocolate, lasagna, pulled pork

Try It with These Recipes: Chicken Wings with Spicy Maple Barbecue Sauce (page 118), Maple-Roasted Parsnips with Pumpkin Seeds (page 175), Grilled Sirloin with Herb & Blue Cheese Compound Butter (page 203)

Also Try: *Sangiovese, Primitivo*

Powerful Reds

TEMPRANILLO

Other Names: Tinta Roriz, Tinto Fino, Tinta del País, Tinto del Toro, Cencibel, Ojo de Llebre, Aragonez

Pronunciation: tem·pra·NEE·yoh

Where It's Made: Spain, Portugal

Recommended Producers: Artadi (Rioja, Spain), Muga (Rioja, Spain), Faustino (Rioja, Spain), Vega Sicilia (Ribera del Duero, Spain)

Overarching Characteristics: Tobacco, leather, plump red fruits, savory herbs, full-bodied, tannic

Tempranillo is a Spanish varietal, although it's also planted across the border in Portugal under the names Tinta Roriz and Aragonez. Tempranillo is also planted in Argentina. It's a big part of the most important regions in Spain: Rioja, Ribera del Duero, and Toro all try to create the best Tempranillo.

Tempranillo has depth and complexity with distinctive plush berries, tobacco, and spiced aromas. Its thick black skin is essential for its concentrated flavor profile and structure. The style of these wines will mostly depend on oak aging. There are two mentalities on this in Spain. Some producers follow traditional methods and use new American oak to age their wines. This gives smoky, vanilla, and coconut aromas. Sometimes the oak presence is so noticeable that it can cover up the varietal identity. Modern winemakers opt for shorter aging periods and the use of neutral, already-used barrels, which imparts less oaky aroma. Historically, throughout Spain but especially in Rioja, the quality of wines was mainly accredited to aging time. Any Gran Reserva would be considered better than any Crianza. Some ambitious winemakers disagree with this system, which doesn't give any credit to specific terroir and grape selection. Tempranillo is usually paired with jamón ibérico and aged sheep cheeses. In both cases, the older the better. The bold wines of Ribeira del Duero, Toro, and Rioja complement the deeply flavorful ibérico ham.

Good with: Grilled meats, lentil soup, roasted Cornish game hen, mild meat curry, aged sheep cheeses, roasted vegetables, polenta, chili, and smokey and starchy foods

Try It with These Recipes: Beef Empanadas (page 172), Roasted Vegetable Chili with Crème Fraîche (page 188)

Also Try: *Grenache, Douro blends, Merlot*

SYRAH

Other Names: Shiraz, Hermitage

Pronunciation: see·RAH

Where It's Made: France and Australia

Recommended Producers: Tyrrell's Wines (Hunter Valley, Australia), Penfolds (Barossa, Australia), Michel Chapoutier (Hermitage, Rhône Valley), Jean-Luc Colombo (Cornas, Rhône Valley), Ogier (Côte-Rôtie, Rhône Valley)

Overarching Characteristics: Black pepper, bold, full-bodied, black fruits, bacon

Syrah and Shiraz are exactly the same grape varietal, but with two completely different expressions. Syrah is the French name and Shiraz is the Aussie term. More than just a synonym, these two names have become a way to differentiate styles even outside of these two countries.

The Rhône Valley is the French homeland for Syrah. You'll find the best expression in the Northern Rhône where it's either used as a single-varietal (Cornas) or blended with small quantities of white grapes (Viognier, Roussanne, and Marsanne) to smoothen out the final product, like in Côte-Rôtie or Hermitage. In the southern part of the Rhône valley, Syrah takes place in more complex blends, with Grenache and Mourvèdre. Some parts of the New World—California, Washington, South Africa, and even within Australia—will use the term Syrah to designate lighter, savory wines with a classic and elegant style. Syrah's aromas vary between smoke, violets, earth, and bacon, but it always has vibrant black fruit aromas and freshly ground black pepper. A great peppery Syrah has the ability to add complexity to your dish, just like adding pepper would. You can try to match this aroma with steak rubs or a pepper sauce.

Australian Shiraz is bolder and full-bodied with heavily concentrated jammy fruit character. It gets beef jerky notes and a very big tannins component; it's a riper, heavier style. The black pepper is replaced by dark chocolate bitterness. Barossa

Valley is the most recognized region for Shirazes. Bolder means you can easily pair it with fatty meats.

Good with: Barbecue, wild boar, beef stew, olives, game, lamb, garlic

Try It with These Recipes: Classic Canadian Poutine (page 122), Molasses Baked Beans with Salt Pork (page 168), Roasted Vegetable Chili with Crème Fraîche (page 188), Barbecue Spareribs (page 210), Smoked Meat Sandwiches with Grilled Vegetables (page 212)

Also Try: Shiraz, Pinotage, Tempranillo, Rhône Valley blends

MOURVÈDRE

Other Names: Monastrell, Alicante, Mataró, Damas Noir

Pronunciation: MOOR·ved·ruh

Where It's Made: South of France and Valencia

Recommended Producers: Domaine Tempier (Bandol, France), Domaine du Vieux Télégraphe (Châteauneuf-du-Pape, France), Domaine de Cristia (Châteauneuf-du-Pape, France), Casa Castillo (Jumilla, Spain), Juan Gil (Jumilla, Spain)

Overarching Characteristics: Rustic, meaty, garrigue (essentially, the woodsy aroma of scrubland), dense, powerful

Native of Spain under the name Monastrell, Mourvèdre is now mostly associated with red blends in the South of France and the unique red wines of Bandol. Mourvèdre needs a lot of sunshine to ripen properly; this is why we mostly find it on the Mediterranean coast. Producers in Spain have been working with this grape as a single-varietal to preserve its old-vine plantings, which have been dwindling in recent years.

Mourvèdre has a strong character, with aromas of herbs, garrigue, game, and leather. It's very identifiable, even within a blend. It's a strong and powerful variety with an opaque purple color and dense structure. Its unique flavors pair well with earthy and smoky foods such as wild mushroom, barbecue, and smoked paprika.

Good with: Tomato tart, paprika, mushrooms, lentils, herbs, sausage, pork

Try It with These Recipes: Gnocchi with Shiitake-Mozzarella Sauce (page 193), Roasted Vegetable Chili with Crème Fraîche (page 188), Eggplant Paprikash (page 192)

Also Try: *Cabernet Sauvignon, Nebbiolo, Tempranillo*

LANGUEDOC-ROUSSILLON

Pronunciation: LAHN·guh·doc ROO·see·yohn

Where It's Made: Languedoc-Roussillon, France

Recommended Producers: Gérard Bertrand (Languedoc-Roussillon, France), Cave de Roquebrun (Saint-Chinian, France), Château Maris (Minervois, France), Domaine Boucabeille (Côtes du Roussillon, France), Domaine Cazes (Côtes du Roussillon, France), Domaine Lafage (Côtes du Roussillon, France), Jeff Carrel (Côtes du Roussillon, France)

Overarching Characteristics: Full-bodied, structured, dense, fruit-forward

The region of Languedoc-Roussillon used to be a bulk wine producer. However, there's been a shift toward quality in recent years, and specific appellations are getting recognized for their wines. Languedoc-Roussillon is all about the blends. You'll rarely find single-varietal wine there. The whole region is a mosaic of terroir, climates, and grape varieties. The soils are complex and intricate, with a mix of granite, sand, limestone, and more. The many valleys and hills create various climatic conditions from cool to warm, depending on the altitude and exposition. From old Grenache to Carignan, Syrah, and even Pinot Noir, these wines can hardly be generalized. They are discoveries waiting to be made.

These are the main appellations to look for: Saint-Chinian, Faugères, Corbières, Minervois-la-Livinière, Maury, Côtes-du-Roussillon. They produce deep, concentrated reds with powerful tannin structure and also incredibly good value.

Good with: Cassoulet, paté, game, herbs, olives, tapas

Try It with These Recipes: Lamb Sliders with Brie (page 171), Smoked Meat Sandwiches with Grilled Vegetables (page 212), Braised Lamb Shanks with Rosemary & Red Wine Sauce (page 214)

Also Try: *Rhône blends, Carignan*

NEBBIOLO

Other Names: Nebieul, Spanna, Chiavennasca

Pronunciation: nehb·BYOH·loh

Where It's Made: Piedmont, Italy

Recommended Producers: Mirafiore (Piedmont, Italy), Conterno (Piedmont, Italy), Gaja (Piedmont, Italy), Poderi Colla (Piedmont, Italy), Pio Cesare (Piedmont, Italy), Proprietà Sperino (Piedmont, Italy)

Overarching Characteristics: Pale orange color, rose, forest floor, truffles, powerful tannins, intense structure

The name Nebbiolo comes from the Italian "Nebbia," which means fog. It refers to the cool morning fogs that cover the Piedmontese hills during harvest season. Nebbiolo is characterized by its pale orange color. It's often called the Pinot Noir of Italy because of this pale color and its ability to make extremely refined and elegant wines. Even the nose is delicate and aromatic with aromas of rose, violets, forest floor, truffles, and tar. However, in terms of palate, it's surprisingly different than on the nose. Nebbiolo is an acquired taste, a full-bodied, high-acidity wine with strong character and intense, merciless tannins.

Nebbiolo loves the warm spots where the snow melts first. You can easily spot the best vineyards just by looking at the Piedmontese hills in spring. Barolo and Barbaresco are the most recognized appellations for Nebbiolo, and also for the most expensive of its kind. They're so powerful that they need at least a decade of aging in the bottle before being drinkable. Thankfully, there are also more affordable and early-drinking options in Langhe, Gattinara, Ghemme, Lessona, and Nebbiolo d'Alba. Alba is notably the white truffle capital of the world. A fragrant risotto with shaved white truffles paired with a Nebbiolo draws out its delicate, aromatic qualities.

Good with: Risotto, mushrooms, carne cruda, truffles, bollito misto, herb-crusted roast lamb

Try It with These Recipes: Wild Mushroom Arancini (page 116), Gnocchi with Shiitake-Mozzarella Sauce (page 193), Cornish Hens with Figs & Walnuts (page 204)

Also Try: Syrah, Aglianico, Sangiovese

AGLIANICO

Other Names: Agliatica, Ellanico, Gnanico, Uva Nera

Pronunciation: ah·lyee·AH·nee·koh

Where It's Made: Southern Italy, Campania, Basilicata

Recommended Producers: Mastroberardino (Taurasi, Italy), Donnachiara (Taurasi, Italy), Cantine del Notaio (Aglianico del Vulture, Italy), Feudi di San Gregorio (Campania, Italy)

Overarching Characteristics: Strong, white pepper, deep black cherries, mineral, high acidity, intense tannins

Aglianico makes firm wines with intensely deep flavors and always a mineral component. Its high acidity and tannins earned it the title of Barolo of the South, which is quite the praise. However, it also has a much deeper garnet color than the brick-shaded Barolos.

Taurasi in Campania and Aglianico del Vulture in Basilicata both have a focus on Aglianico. What they have in common is the presence of volcanic soils. This gives the wines distinctive dark mineral character and a lovely complexity.

Meat is a big part of the cuisine in Basilicata. The meaty notes of Aglianico are a great match for a number of meats, including deeply flavored prime rib, venison, rabbit, and oxtail.

Good with: Burgers, buffalo wings, oxtail, deer, mushrooms, beans

Try It with These Recipes: Gnocchi with Shiitake-Mozzarella Sauce (page 193), Chicken Cacciatore (page 206)

Also Try: *Negroamaro, Cabernet Sauvignon, Tannat, Nebbiolo*

MALBEC

Other Names: Cot, Auxerrois, Pressac, Pied Rouge, Jacobian, Grifforin

Pronunciation: MAAL·bek

Where It's Made: Argentina, Cahors

Recommended Producers: Catena Zapata (Mendoza, Argentina), Colomé (Salta, Argentina), Achaval Ferrer (Mendoza, Argentina), Terrazas de los Andes (Mendoza, Argentina), Zuccardi (Mendoza, Argentina), Georges Vigouroux (Cahors, France), Clos Triguedina (Cahors, France)

Overarching Characteristics: Magenta color, blueberries, cocoa, smoke, high alcohol, dense tannins

Originally, Malbec was popular in France until the 19th century. Once an important part of Bordeaux blends, now many Bordeaux producers shiver at the very mention of the grape. The only French region still linked to Malbec is Cahors, with their black wines. In a way, Argentina saved Malbec, as it would almost be forgotten without it. It became a superstar in Argentina in the 1990s and Mendoza has been proven able to give this varietal a second chance at being included in the popular international varietals. South Africa, Australia, Chile, and the United States followed Mendoza's lead and started to plant Malbec again, mostly for their red blends.

Malbec is distinguishable by its dark, almost opaque color with fuchsia hue. It has aromas of fleshy, almost chewy black fruits and berries, pomegranate, blueberries, and chocolate as well as a smoky character. Medium- to-full-bodied, Malbec has a high alcohol level and very dense tannins—a natural match for Argentinian beef empanadas.

Good with: Garlic, rosemary, lean meats, shallots, mushrooms, endives, Cajun, red meats

Try It with These Recipes: Beef Empanadas (page 172), Berry-Glazed Duck Breasts (page 208), Braised Lamb Shanks with Rosemary & Red Wine Sauce (page 214)

Also Try: Syrah, Touriga Nacional, Petit Verdot, Petite Sirah

PORTUGUESE BLENDS

Where It's Made: Portugal

Recommended Producers: Duas Quintas (Douro, Portugal), Casa Ferreirinha (Douro, Portugal), Quinta do Vesuvio (Douro, Portugal), Mouchão (Alentejo, Portugal), Campolargo (Bairrada, Portugal)

Overarching Characteristics: Deep red and black fruits, concentration, robust

The unique character of Portuguese wine relies on blends. This mix of grapes is part of the tradition and winemaking heritage of Portugal. Not so long ago, it was said that even winemakers didn't knew what was planted in their vineyards and **field blends** (vineyards with various grape varietals all mingled together) were the norm. Sometimes you'll find this information on the back label.

DOURO VALLEY: The Douro Valley is unmistakably the most popular and recognized region. They produce deep robust red wines with depth, concentration, and firm tannins.

ALENTEJO: This southern region is warm and produces rich wines with lots of fruit character and body. It's full-bodied and rounded.

BAIRRADA: Situated near the Atlantic Coast, the region is known for the Baga variety. The refreshing ocean breeze makes it softer but still full-bodied and high acid with textured tannins. Baga's acidity enables it to pair with some seafood like grilled octopus.

DÃO: This region benefits from higher altitudes. It produces elegant wines, with good acidity, complexity, and balance.

Good with: Grilled sardines, garlic, game, lamb, beef, pork, thyme, strong and hard cheeses

Try It with These Recipes: Molasses Baked Beans with Salt Pork (page 168), Lamb Sliders with Brie (page 171), Beef Empanadas (page 172), Braised Lamb Shanks with Rosemary & Red Wine Sauce (page 214)

Also Try: *Trás-os-Montes, Castelão, Jaen*

CABERNET SAUVIGNON

Other Names: Petit Cabernet, Vidure, Uva Francese

Pronunciation: kab·er·NAY soh·vin·YOHN.

Where It's Made: Worldwide

Recommended Producers: Heitz (Napa Valley, California), Harlan Estate (Napa Valley, California) Château Ducru-Beaucaillou (Saint Julien, Bordeaux), Château Haut-Bailly (Graves, Bordeaux), Wynns Coonawarra Estate (Coonawarra, Australia), Carmen (Maipo Valley, Chile)

Overarching Characteristics: Cassis, pencil shavings, intense tannins, bold

Cabernet Sauvignon is always the first example that comes in mind in terms of a powerful, heavy red wine variety. It's loved and cherished for its concentration and ageability. It became widely planted throughout the world for its tough wood and easy-to-grow ability. It can withstand extreme temperatures and many diseases.

Cabernet Sauvignon wines are usually opaque and slightly purple with black fruit aromas and cassis and vegetal notes (including mint, eucalyptus, and green bell pepper). On the palate, it has moderate acidity but very high tannins and alcohol. Some areas may show regional character, but Cabernet Sauvignon is mostly influenced by oak aging and often has vanilla and clove characteristics. When it comes to reds, Cabernet Sauvignon is pretty much the most powerful wine you can find—you'll want this with the aged steak you bring home from the butcher.

BORDEAUX: Cabernet Sauvignon is the star of left bank Bordeaux. It's the main component of all the most luxurious châteaux. The gravelly soils are ideal for age-worthy, intense red wine expressions.

CALIFORNIA: New World Cabernet, especially in Napa and Sonoma, focus more on plush blackberry and black currant fruit as well as rich notes like licorice. You'll always find great depth and concentration as well as cedar and tobacco notes from extended oak-aging treatment.

SOUTH AUSTRALIA: Coonawarra has very unique red clay soils called terra rossa. It produces some of the most powerful Cabernet in the world, with very distinctive character and great quality for a fraction of Bordeaux prices.

CHILE: If you're looking for good value Cabernet Sauvignon, Chile delivers. Chilean Cabernet Sauvignon often has a distinctive minty character.

Good with: Red meats with heavy fat, beef, lamb, old cheeses, bitter chocolate, pepper

Try It with These Recipes: Barbecue Spareribs (page 210), Smoked Meat Sandwiches with Grilled Vegetables (page 212), Grilled Sirloin with Herb & Blue Cheese Compound Butter (page 203), Filet Mignon with Coffee-Chocolate Sauce (page 218)

Also Try: *Merlot, Aglianico, Syrah*

BORDEAUX BLENDS

Pronunciation: bor·DOE

Where It's Made: Worldwide

Recommended Producers: VIK (Cachapoal Valley, Chile), Reyneke (Stellenbosch, South Africa), Te Mata (Hawke's Bay, New Zealand), Vérité (Sonoma, California), Vasse Felix (Margaret River, Australia), Château Rauzan-Ségla (Margaux, Bordeaux), Château Léoville-Poyferré (Saint Julien, Bordeaux), Château Cos d'Estournel (Saint Estèphe, Bordeaux)

Overarching Characteristics: Black fruit, tight tannins, structure, ageability

Cabernet Sauvignon, Merlot, Cabernet Franc, Malbec, and Petit Verdot—these are the grapes that make the noble blends of Bordeaux. This region was so prized and envied that it's been imitated throughout the world, thus the use of Bordeaux blend globally. Normally, Bordeaux blends will have at least two of the original grape varietals, but it can also include locally planted grapes. Chilean Bordeaux blends include Carménère, Australian Bordeaux blends include Shiraz, and Tuscan Bordeaux blends may include Sangiovese.

There are no rules surrounding this term outside of Bordeaux. It's just so widely recognizable and easy to understand that it's become common language. The goal is not necessary to copy Bordeaux. Each region has its own distinctive style, but it's a synonym for a full-bodied red blend built to age.

Good with: Fatty meats, steak

Try It with These Recipes: Eggplant Paprikash (page 192), Chicken Cacciatore (page 206), Barbecue Spareribs (page 210), Braised Lamb Shanks with Rosemary & Red Wine Sauce (page 214)

Also Try: *Super Tuscans, Merlot, Cabernet Sauvignon*

TANNAT

Other Names: Madiran, Harriague, Moustrou

Pronunciation: tan·AT

Where It's Made: Madiran and Uruguay

Recommended Producers: Château Montus (Madiran, France), Château Bouscassé (Madiran, France), Bodega Garzón (Uruguay)

Overarching Characteristics: Opaque, spicy, licorice, textured, powerful

Tannat wines are as deep and opaque as it can get. Just by looking at a Tannat wine, you know what to expect. It has boldness and concentration, with aromas of vanilla, black fruits, licorice, dark roasted coffee, cardamom, and spices. Its tannins are extremely tight and grippy, making it a very textured wine.

The only place to still find it in France is in Madiran, and in small quantities in surrounding southwest appellations like Irouléguy, Tursan, and Béarn. The region's definitely under the radar, even almost forgotten. Fortunately, it has also found a place in Italy and in the New World—in Argentina, Australia, Brazil, Peru, and the United States. Most prominently, Tannat is the most planted grape in Uruguay.

Good with: Braised beef, duck, game, stews

Try It with These Recipes: Beef Empanadas (page 172), Berry-Glazed Duck Breasts (page 208)

Also Try: *Malbec, Tempranillo, Cabernet Sauvignon*

Heirloom
Tomato & Peach
Bruschetta
(page 110),
PAIR WITH: Rosé,
page 66

Crab Cakes with
Tangerine Salsa
(page 158),
PAIR WITH:
Sparkling Wine,
page 21

Chilled Zucchini
Noodles with
Coconut-Peanut
Sauce (page 181),
PAIR WITH:
Aromatic Whites,
page 57

PART II

THE FOOD

You don't *need* wine with your food, and you don't
have to have food with your wine, but the right match
will open your eyes to an enhanced eating and drinking
experience that is so much greater than the sum of its
parts. Unlock the world of flavors with recipes and pairing
recommendations that were made for each other.

Heirloom Tomato &
Peach Bruschetta (page 110),
PAIR WITH: Rosé,
page 66

Chapter 5

Snacks, Nibbles & Sweets

WINE PAIRING GUIDE

○
Sparkling Wines
Sweet & Fortified Wines

○
Crisp & Edgy Whites
Aromatic Whites
Rich & Bold Whites
Rosé Wines

●
Delicate Reds
Friendly, Moderate Reds
Powerful Reds

Garlic-Parmesan Roasted Edamame

PAIR WITH:
◯ Crisp & Edgy Whites

SERVES 4 / PREP TIME: 5 MINUTES / **COOK TIME:** 50 MINUTES

Upcycle frozen edamame by roasting them with umami-rich Parmesan cheese and garlic powder, then say hello to your new favorite drinking snack. These crunchy, addictive, salty bites will keep you reaching for your glass of wine. Try a white with bright acidity and some herbaceous notes to complement the edamame. A cool Vinho Verde would fit the bill, as would a crisp Grüner Veltliner, a Verdejo, or even an aromatic white such as Torrontés. Use the edamame straight from the freezer (do not thaw); otherwise, they will steam instead of roast.

1 (12-ounce) package frozen shelled edamame	½ teaspoon garlic powder	¼ cup grated Parmesan cheese
	¼ teaspoon sea salt	

1. Preheat the oven to 375°F. Line a baking sheet with parchment paper.

2. In a large bowl, put the edamame. Add the garlic powder and sea salt and stir to combine. Spread the mixture on the baking sheet and bake, stirring halfway through, until the edamame are crispy and lightly browned, about 50 minutes.

3. Remove from oven and sprinkle the Parmesan cheese over the edamame. Stir to combine. Serve immediately. Store in an airtight container at room temperature for up to 5 days.

Bacon-Asiago Popcorn

PAIR WITH:
Sparkling Wines

SERVES 4 / PREP TIME: 10 MINUTES / **COOK TIME:** 10 MINUTES

There's a reason why popcorn is the ultimate bar snack. It's light, crunchy, a great vehicle for salt, and it alternates beautifully with sips of wine. This popcorn is all that but supercharged with crunchy homemade bacon bits and the salty tang of shredded cheese. A nice sparkling wine will match the popcorn's delicate crunch, and the acidity will quench your thirst after all that salinity. Try a Chardonnay-based sparkling, like a Blanc de Blancs Champagne, or a Crémant de Jura. The richer and creamier the sparkling, the better, as it will harmonize with the rich Asiago and bacon.

8 slices bacon, cut into ¼-inch pieces

2 tablespoons extra-virgin olive oil, or

1 tablespoon bacon fat and 1 tablespoon extra-virgin olive oil

¼ cup popcorn kernels

¼ cup shredded Asiago cheese

Sea salt

1. In a large skillet over medium-high heat, sauté the bacon until crispy and cooked through, about 6 minutes. Using a slotted spoon, transfer the bacon bits to a paper towel–lined plate. Reserve 1 tablespoon of bacon fat (if using).

2. In a medium stockpot, heat the oil over medium-high heat. Pour a few kernels into the pot and cover it with a lid. When the test kernels pop, add the remaining kernels, cover and cook, gently shaking the saucepan until all the kernels are popped, about 4 minutes.

3. Remove from the heat and transfer to a bowl. Add the bacon and Asiago and stir to combine. Season with salt to taste and serve.

Sweet & Spicy Candied Pecans

PAIR WITH:
Sweet & Fortified Wines

MAKES 2 CUPS / PREP TIME: 10 MINUTES / **COOK TIME:** 15 MINUTES

When paired with Madeira, these sweet-hot seasoned nuts are a match made in heaven. The sweeter style from Boal and Malmsey matches the toasty brown sugar flavor of the pecans while softening the heat. Another great pairing is a rich 20-year-old tawny port, which enhances the caramel flavors and mellows the cayenne. These pecans are excellent as a snack and make a great topping for a soup or salad.

2 tablespoons brown sugar

1 tablespoon extra-virgin olive oil

1 teaspoon ground cinnamon

¼ teaspoon sea salt

⅛ to ¼ teaspoon cayenne pepper

2 cups raw pecans

1. Preheat the oven to 350°F. Line a baking sheet with parchment paper.

2. In a medium bowl, stir together the brown sugar, oil, cinnamon, salt, and cayenne pepper until well combined. Add the pecans and stir until the nuts are well coated. Transfer the nuts to the baking sheet and spread in a single layer.

3. Bake, stirring frequently, until the pecans are golden brown and caramelized, about 15 minutes.

4. Remove from oven and let cool. Break the pecans apart, if necessary, and serve.

5. Store the pecans in an airtight container at room temperature for up to 2 weeks.

SOMM TIP: These candied pecans are the perfect accompaniment for your favorite cheese board.

Bacon-Wrapped Dates with Goat Cheese

PAIR WITH:
Sparkling Wines, Sweet & Fortified Wines

SERVES 8 / **PREP TIME:** 15 MINUTES / **COOK TIME:** 18 MINUTES

On their own, Medjool dates are a sweet, fudgy indulgence. When stuffed with goat cheese, wrapped in bacon, and baked, the already-rich fruit becomes even more glorious. For a flavor bomb like this, try a bubbly rosé, either Cava, Champagne, or a sparkling from California. The acidity from the wine will cleanse the palate and prime it for another bite. Another option would be Madeira, to balance the saltiness and sweetness.

1 (4-ounce) package soft goat cheese, at room temperature	24 whole pitted Medjool dates	12 slices bacon, preferably applewood-smoked, cut crosswise into 2 pieces

1. Preheat the oven to 400°F. Line a baking sheet with parchment paper.

2. Using a teaspoon, stuff the cheese into the open end of each date, about 1 teaspoon per date. Wrap half a piece of bacon around each date and arrange on the baking sheet, with the end of the bacon piece facing down. Bake until the bacon is crispy, turning the dates over halfway through, 15 to 18 minutes. Serve hot.

Beet Carpaccio & Goat Cheese with Pink Grapefruit Dressing

PAIR WITH:
● Rosé Wines ● Friendly, Moderate Reds

SERVES 4 / PREP TIME: 30 MINUTES, PLUS 30 MINUTES MARINATING TIME

This vegetarian riff on carpaccio, an Italian appetizer of thinly sliced raw beef spritzed with lemon juice, subs in paper-thin slivers of beets for the meat, along with a grapefruit dressing, rich goat cheese, and walnuts. This light, flavorful dish is a perfect fit for a refreshing Bandol Rosé, which has the acidity to match the citrus. To play up the dish's earthiness, try a bottle of Mourvèdre for its wild aromas. For red options, pair with a Chinon or Bourgueil, both Cabernet Franc–based wines from the Loire Valley. The earthy character of these wines will match that of the beets. To make this dish the most colorful it can be, use a mix of red, golden, and candy cane beets.

8 small beets, peeled and trimmed, sliced paper-thin

¼ cup freshly squeezed pink grapefruit juice, divided

2 tablespoons extra-virgin olive oil

1 teaspoon honey

½ teaspoon chopped fresh thyme

Sea salt

1 cup microgreens, such as baby arugula or pea shoots

½ cup soft goat cheese

¼ cup chopped walnuts or pecans (toasted, if desired)

1. Arrange the beet slices in slightly overlapping circles on 4 plates. In a small bowl, whisk together 3 tablespoons of grapefruit juice, the oil, honey, and thyme. Drizzle the dressing over the beets and season with salt. Set aside for 30 minutes at room temperature.

2. In a medium bowl, combine the microgreens with the remaining 1 tablespoon of grapefruit juice. Place a quarter of the greens on the center of each plate. Sprinkle with the goat cheese and nuts. Serve.

PREPARATION TIP: A mandoline is the best tool to use when slicing food incredibly thin. Just make sure you use the guard to protect your fingers.

Shrimp Ceviche
with Cucumber & Avocado

PAIR WITH:
Crisp & Edgy Whites

SERVES 6 / PREP TIME: 20 MINUTES, PLUS 1 TO 2 HOURS MARINATING TIME

This Peruvian seafood cocktail is as refreshing as they come: tender shrimp "cooked" in citrus juice, cooling cucumbers, creamy avocado, sharp onion and chile, and juicy tomatoes. The taste is vibrant and fresh, and the wine should be, too. The green flavors of cucumber and avocado shine when paired with New Zealand's Sauvignon Blanc. Another Sauvignon, like a mineral-driven Sancerre, would also be a good match.

1 pound raw shrimp, peeled, deveined, and chopped

Juice of 5 limes (about ¾ cup)

Juice of 1 lemon

Juice of 1 orange

1 English cucumber, chopped into ¼-inch chunks

2 medium tomatoes, seeded and chopped

½ small red onion, finely chopped

1 jalapeño pepper, seeded and minced (optional)

2 tablespoons chopped fresh cilantro

Sea salt

1 large avocado, chopped

Tostadas or tortilla chips, for serving

1. Put the shrimp and lime, lemon, and orange juices in a large bowl. Stir to combine. Cover and refrigerate for about 1 hour to "cook" the shrimp, stirring once or twice. The shrimp should be opaque but still tender.

2. Add the cucumber, tomatoes, onion, pepper, and cilantro to the shrimp mixture and stir to combine. Season with salt to taste. Stir in the avocado and serve immediately with chips or over tostadas.

COOKING TIP: The shrimp will continue to "cook" as they sit in the lime juice, and the seafood will eventually get tough and unpalatable. This dish is best eaten immediately. If you are leery of the raw shrimp, poach the shrimp until just cooked, cool, and add to the other ingredients. The dish will not have to sit if using cooked shrimp.

Heirloom Tomato & Peach Bruschetta

PAIR WITH:

● Rosé Wines ● Sparkling Wines ● Aromatic Whites

SERVES 4 / **PREP TIME:** 20 MINUTES / **COOK TIME:** 2 MINUTES

Capture the taste of peak summer in this bruschetta, which combines the most flavorful tomatoes—heirlooms—with the fleeting nectar of ripe peaches, and salty crumbles of Manchego cheese. A Provençal Rosé, a light Pinot Grigio, a crisp Cava, or even a heavier white Côtes du Roussillon all have enough acidity to pair with the tomatoes, and if they have a slight touch of sweetness, it can enhance the flavor of the peaches.

3 medium heirloom tomatoes, seeded and chopped

2 peaches, chopped

⅓ cup extra-virgin olive oil, divided

2 tablespoons chopped fresh basil

1 tablespoon freshly squeezed lime juice

Sea salt

1 baguette, preferably sourdough, cut into ½-inch-thick slices on a bias

3 ounces Manchego cheese (about ¾ cup), crumbled

1. Preheat the oven to broil.

2. In a medium bowl, combine the tomatoes, peaches, 2 tablespoons of oil, basil, and lime juice and mix well. Season with salt to taste.

3. Brush the baguette slices with the remaining 3 tablespoons of oil and place them on a baking sheet. Toast on both sides, turning the slices over halfway through, about 1 minute. Spoon the tomato mixture onto each slice and sprinkle with the cheese. Broil for 30 seconds longer or until the cheese is melted; serve immediately

SERVING TIP: The bruschetta mixture can be used as a dip, or served with tortilla or pita chips.

Caramelized Onion Tart with Feta Cheese & Pine Nuts

PAIR WITH:
Aromatic Whites, Rich & Bold Whites

SERVES 4 / PREP TIME: 40 MINUTES / COOK TIME: 55 MINUTES

The inspiration for this dish is the classic Provençal tart called pissaladière, a rustic flatbread topped with anchovies, olives, and caramelized onions. What this rendition lacks in little salty fish and olives, it makes up for in sweet onions and brined feta cheese. A PSA—caramelized onions take a long time to cook down, and it's totally worth your time. Choose a wine that stands up to the tart's richness and even brightens it up a bit, such as an off-dry Gewürztraminer from Alsace, a smoky oaked Sauvignon Blanc like Fumé Blanc, or a Pouilly-Fumé, which has high acidity and good body.

2 tablespoons extra-virgin olive oil

2 large Vidalia or other sweet onions, thinly sliced

¼ teaspoon sea salt

1 (8-ounce) puff pastry sheet, thawed

4 ounces feta cheese, crumbled

¼ cup pine nuts

1 teaspoon chopped fresh thyme

1. In a large skillet, heat the oil over medium heat. Add the onions, sautéing until lightly browned, about 10 minutes. Reduce the heat to low, add the salt and cook, stirring occasionally, until the onions are jammy and caramelized, about 25 minutes. Add a couple of tablespoons of water if the skillet dries out.

2. Preheat the oven at 400°F.

3. Unfold the puff pastry sheet and roll it out into a 10-by-14-inch rectangle. Line a baking sheet with parchment paper, lay the puff pastry on it, prick the sheet all over with a fork, and set aside.

4. Spread the onions in an even layer over the pastry, leaving about an inch at the edges. Sprinkle the feta and pine nuts over the onions. Bake until the crust is golden, 18 to 20 minutes. Top the tart with thyme, cut it into 8 pieces, and serve warm or at room temperature.

Fig, Camembert & Arugula Flatbreads

PAIR WITH:
● Sparkling Wines ● Aromatic Whites

SERVES 4 / PREP TIME: 10 MINUTES / **COOK TIME:** 15 MINUTES

These flatbreads were genetically engineered to make you crave wine—jammy figs, melty Camembert, nutty pecans, and peppery arugula on toasted flatbread. The arugula has a bitter note that pairs well with something crisp, whereas a soft cheese like Camembert asks for acidity to cut through the creaminess. A classic pairing would have bubbles, like a Crémant de Loire or Vouvray Mousseux. A Riesling from Eden Valley in Australia—aromatic and vibrant, with generous, rich aromas—would also be a great match.

2 flatbreads, such as naan or pita

1 tablespoon extra-virgin olive oil

4 ounces Camembert cheese, thinly sliced

6 fresh figs, quartered

¼ cup chopped pecans

½ cup baby arugula

1. Preheat oven to 400°F. Line a baking sheet with parchment paper.

2. Brush the flatbreads with oil and put them on the baking sheet. Arrange the cheese on the flatbreads, then place the figs on top. Bake until the cheese is melted and the figs are tender and lightly caramelized, about 15 minutes. Remove from the oven and sprinkle on the pecans and arugula. Cut into quarters and serve immediately.

INGREDIENT TIP: If you only have dried figs available, rehydrate them by simmering the fruit gently in water for about 10 minutes. Drain on a paper towel–lined plate, quarter, and use in the recipe.

Lemony Onion Rings

SERVES 4 / PREP TIME: 15 MINUTES / **COOK TIME:** 15 MINUTES

Food doesn't need to be fancy to cry out for Champagne. Such is the case with these crisp, batter-fried onion rings. The high acidity of Champagne balances the richness of the deep-fried batter and matches its yeasty flavors. Beyond France, consider a Sekt or a crisp sparkling wine from the Finger Lakes. For dunking, there's nothing better than mayo.

1 cup all-purpose flour

2 large eggs, lightly beaten

¾ cup water, plus more as needed

2 tablespoons freshly squeezed lemon juice

1¼ teaspoon sea salt

1 teaspoon baking powder

1 large sweet onion, sliced very thin (about ⅛-½ inch)

Canola oil, for frying

1. In a large bowl, whisk together the flour, eggs, water, lemon juice, salt, and baking powder until a smooth pancake-like batter forms. If the batter is too thick, add water by the tablespoon until you've achieved the right consistency.

2. In a large heavy-bottomed saucepan, heat 3 inches of oil to 375°F. (A pinch of flour will sizzle when added to the oil.)

3. Separate the onion rings, dip into the batter in small batches, and fry, turning, until golden brown and crispy on all sides, about 3 minutes. Remove with tongs or a slotted spoon and drain on a paper towel–lined plate. Serve immediately.

Crispy Shrimp with Romesco Sauce

PAIR WITH:
● Friendly, Moderate Reds

SERVES 4 / PREP TIME: 25 MINUTES **/ COOK TIME:** 30 MINUTES

Romesco sauce, a traditional Catalan puree of roasted peppers, almonds, tomatoes, vinegar, and garlic, calls for an equally flavorsome red wine. (Yes, even when served with shrimp.) Try a Cabernet Franc from the Loire Valley or a Côtes du Rhône, which will highlight the roasted flavor of the peppers. Spoon any leftover sauce over the vegetables, such as steamed asparagus or grilled scallions.

FOR THE SAUCE

¼ cup extra-virgin olive oil, divided

1 thick slice crusty bread, torn into ½-inch chunks

½ cup slivered almonds

2 teaspoons minced garlic

1 (15-ounce) can whole, peeled tomatoes (preferably San Marzano), drained

1 cup (8-ounces) chopped roasted red peppers

¼ cup chopped fresh parsley

1 tablespoon Sherry wine vinegar

1 teaspoon smoked paprika

¼ teaspoon sea salt

⅛ teaspoon cayenne pepper (optional)

FOR THE SHRIMP

¾ cup all-purpose flour

¼ teaspoon garlic powder

2 large eggs

2 cups panko bread crumbs

½ teaspoon dried parsley

½ teaspoon dried basil

¼ teaspoon sea salt

1 pound extra-large (26 to 30 count) shrimp, peeled and deveined

Nonstick olive oil cooking spray

1. To make the sauce: In a medium skillet, heat 1 tablespoon of oil over medium heat. Sauté the bread and almonds until lightly browned, about 3 minutes. Add the garlic and sauté until softened, about 2 minutes.

2. Transfer the mixture to a food processor and add the remaining 3 tablespoons of oil, the tomatoes, red pepper, parsley, vinegar, paprika, salt, and cayenne pepper (if using) and puree until smooth.

3. Transfer to a serving bowl. (Any sauce not used on the shrimp can be stored in an airtight container in the refrigerator for up to 1 week or in the freezer for up to 1 month.)

4. To make the shrimp: Preheat the oven to 400°F. Line a baking sheet with parchment paper.

5. In a bowl, combine the flour and garlic powder. In a second bowl, beat the eggs. In a third bowl, combine the bread crumbs, parsley, basil, and salt. Dredge the shrimp in the flour mixture, then the egg, then the bread-crumb mixture. Place the breaded shrimp on the baking sheet. Repeat with the remaining shrimp, placing them in a single layer. Lightly coat with the cooking spray and bake until golden brown and crispy, 12 to 15 minutes.

Wild Mushroom Arancini

PAIR WITH:
● Delicate Reds, Powerful Reds

SERVES 4 / PREP TIME: 30 MINUTES, PLUS COOLING TIME / **COOK TIME:** 43 MINUTES

These fried croquettes are the gift that keep giving. When you bite through the crisp exterior, what you find is a hot filling of mushroom risotto with a melted mozzarella center. Pair it with a red wine with good acidity, such as Pinot Noir or Poulsard, which will counter the creaminess of the risotto while complementing the mushrooms' umami flavors. Nebbiolo wines such as Langhe or a Barbaresco are also a good match. If you have leftover risotto, reheat it with a little broth in a small skillet and eat it for dinner.

3 cups low-sodium chicken broth

1 ounce dried wild mushrooms (about 1 cup)

3 tablespoons butter, divided

1 onion, finely chopped

2 teaspoons minced garlic

1½ cups chopped fresh mushrooms, such as shiitake, oyster, or maitake

1 cup Arborio rice

½ cup dry white wine

½ cup Parmesan cheese

12 (½-inch) cubes mozzarella cheese

1 cup all-purpose flour

2 large eggs

1½ cups panko bread crumbs

Canola oil, for frying

1. Line a baking sheet with parchment paper and set aside. In a medium saucepan, bring the broth and wild mushrooms to a boil over medium-high heat. Strain out the rehydrated mushrooms, chop, and set aside in a bowl. Reduce the heat to low so the broth simmers gently.

2. In a large saucepan, melt 2 tablespoons of butter over medium-high heat. Sauté the onion and garlic until softened, about 3 minutes. Add the fresh mushrooms and sauté until they are lightly browned, 6 to 7 minutes. Stir in the rice to toast lightly, about 4 minutes. Add the wine and deglaze the pan, scraping any cooked bits from the bottom. Bring the mixture to a boil and cook until the wine is absorbed into the rice, about 2 minutes.

3. Add a ladleful of simmering broth to the rice, stirring constantly, until the liquid is absorbed. Repeat this process until all the broth used up or the rice is tender but al dente, 18 to 20 minutes. Remove from the heat.

4. Stir the rehydrated mushrooms, Parmesan cheese, and the remaining 1 tablespoon of butter into the risotto. Spread the hot risotto on the baking sheet to cool at room temperature.

5. When the risotto is cool, scoop up the rice and roll it into balls about 1½ inches in diameter. Press a piece of mozzarella cheese into each ball and enclose the cheese. Put the finished balls on a plate and refrigerate for at least 30 minutes.

6. Pour the flour in a bowl. Crack the eggs into another bowl and beat lightly. Pour the panko in a third bowl. Dredge the rice balls in the flour, then the egg, and then the bread crumb mixture. Place them on a baking sheet.

7. In a large heavy-bottomed saucepan, heat 3 inches of oil to 375°F. (A pinch of flour will sizzle when added to the oil.) Fry the arancini in small batches until they're golden brown, turning to get all the sides, about 3 minutes. Remove with a slotted spoon and drain on a paper towel–lined plate. Serve immediately.

COOKING TIP: To make ahead, freeze arancini for up to 3 months, thaw in the refrigerator overnight, and reheat at 400°F for 20 minutes.

Chicken Wings with Spicy Maple Barbecue Sauce

PAIR WITH:
⚪ Aromatic Whites ⚫ Friendly, Moderate Reds

SERVES 6 / PREP TIME: 15 MINUTES **/ COOK TIME:** 40 MINUTES

Wings are the perfect finger food. Add a sticky sauce with a touch of heat and you're in bar snack heaven. This sweet-spicy mix is the perfect excuse to open a fantastic off-dry Riesling, a bold Zinfandel, or even an Amarone, as long as there's residual sugar to match the sweetness. Serve with a creamy blue cheese sauce and crisp, cut veggies for a classic wing experience. Blue cheese also works great with these sweeter wines, and the creaminess can help manage the high alcohol of Zinfandel. Perfect in every way!

FOR THE WINGS

4 pounds chicken wings, cut into drumettes and flats	½ cup all-purpose flour Sea salt	Nonstick olive oil cooking spray

FOR THE SAUCE

1 tablespoon extra-virgin olive oil	1 cup unsweetened apple juice	2 tablespoons apple cider vinegar
½ sweet onion, chopped	1 cup maple syrup	2 tablespoons hot sauce
2 teaspoons minced garlic	¼ cup tomato paste	¼ teaspoon sea salt

1. To make the wings: Preheat the oven to 425°F. Line a baking sheet with parchment paper.

2. Pat the chicken wings dry with paper towels and put them in a large bowl. Combine with the flour and season with salt. Spread the wings in one layer on the baking sheet, shaking off any excess flour, and spray with the cooking spray on both sides. Bake until golden brown and crispy, turning once, 35 to 40 minutes. Remove from oven and transfer to a large bowl.

3. To make the sauce: In a large saucepan, heat the oil over medium-high heat. Sauté the onion and garlic until softened, about 3 minutes. Stir in the apple juice, maple syrup, tomato paste, vinegar, and hot sauce and bring to a boil. Reduce the heat to low and simmer for 30 minutes, stirring occasionally, until the sauce coats the back of a spoon. Pour the sauce over the wings and toss to coat. Serve hot.

> **COOKING TIP:** If you like your wings drier, bake the sauced wings in a single layer on the baking for 10 minutes at 425°F. They will be sticky and lightly charred on the edges.

Pomegranate-Glazed Turkey Meatballs

PAIR WITH:

● Friendly, Moderate Reds

SERVES 8 / PREP TIME: 15 MINUTES / **COOK TIME:** 40 MINUTES

Fruit-glazed meatballs are deliciously retro. This updated version uses tart pomegranate juice with a little honey and warm spices instead of sugary jam as the glaze. A classic pairing with meatballs is Sangiovese. The rustic tannins of a Chianti Classico, plus its vibrant red fruits and acidity, will work great with the richness of the meat and the pomegranate flavor. Or try a fruity Spanish Garnacha. Look for "old vines," as the added complexity and rich texture will complement the dish.

FOR THE POMEGRANATE GLAZE

1 teaspoon extra-virgin olive oil

½ sweet onion, finely chopped

1¼ cups pure pomegranate juice

2 teaspoons honey

⅛ teaspoon ground cloves

Sea salt

FOR THE MEATBALLS

1 pound extra-lean ground turkey

½ cup panko bread crumbs

1 large egg

3 tablespoons minced shallot

2 tablespoons chopped fresh parsley

1 tablespoon chopped fresh basil

1 teaspoon minced garlic

¼ teaspoon sea salt

Nonstick olive oil cooking spray

1. To make the pomegranate glaze: In a small saucepan, heat the oil over medium-high heat. Sauté the onion until very tender, about 5 minutes. Add the pomegranate juice, honey, and cloves and bring to a boil. Reduce the heat to low and simmer until the glaze thickens and reduces by half, about 20 minutes. Season with salt, remove from the heat, and set aside.

2. To make the meatballs: Preheat oven to 400°F. Line a baking sheet with parchment paper. In a large bowl, mix the turkey, bread crumbs, egg, shallot, parsley, basil, garlic, and salt until well combined. Form into 1-inch meatballs and place on the baking sheet. Spray with the cooking spray and bake until cooked through and lightly browned, about 20 minutes.

3. Transfer to a large bowl and add the glaze. Stir to coat and transfer to a serving dish. Store leftovers in the refrigerator in an airtight container for up to 3 days.

Classic Canadian Poutine

PAIR WITH:
● Delicate Reds

SERVES 4 / PREP TIME: 30 MINUTES, PLUS CHILLING TIME / **COOK TIME:** 35 MINUTES

Poutine, a Quebecois truck-stop staple, is a culinary triumph: melty cheese, salty gravy, and crispy fries in each bite. A Burgundian Pinot Noir can amplify the flavors of the gravy and lighten the dish, while the acidity cuts through the cheese curds. The trick to keeping the fries crisp under all that gravy is to double-fry them.

2 pounds russet potatoes, cut into ¼-inch batons

4 tablespoons unsalted butter

¼ cup all-purpose flour

4 cups good-quality, low-sodium beef broth (homemade, if possible)

Canola oil, for frying

Sea salt

Freshly ground black pepper

3 cups cheese curds

1. Put the potatoes in a bowl and cover with cold water. Refrigerate for at least 1 hour.

2. In a large saucepan, melt the butter over medium-high heat. Add the flour and whisk continually until the mixture is a light golden brown, about 5 minutes. Whisk in the broth and bring to a boil. Reduce the heat to low and simmer, whisking continually, until the gravy is thick and smooth, about 5 minutes. Remove from heat and cover to keep warm.

3. In a large heavy-bottomed saucepan, heat 3 inches of oil to 350°F. (A pinch of flour will sizzle when added to the oil.) Drain the potatoes and pat them completely dry with paper towels. Working in small batches, fry the potatoes until tender but not browned, about 5 minutes. Put the fries on a paper towel–lined plate to drain and repeat until all the fries are cooked. Increase the oil temperature to 350°F and, working in small batches again, fry the potatoes until very crispy and golden brown, about 3 minutes. Remove with a slotted spoon, drain on a paper towel–lined plate, and repeat with the remaining potatoes. Season the fries with salt and pepper, divide among 4 plates, and top with the cheese curds and hot gravy.

| **SERVING TIP:** Use store-bought frozen fries to save time on prep.

Banana-Cinnamon Bread Pudding

PAIR WITH:
Sweet & Fortified Wines

SERVES 8 / PREP TIME: 10 MINUTES, PLUS 30 MINUTES TO 1 HOUR SOAKING TIME /
COOK TIME: 1 HOUR

Nothing says comfort like steaming-hot bread pudding. This one, perfumed with bananas, cinnamon, and vanilla, is especially homey. Late-harvest wines tend to have tropical notes that are a good match for the bananas' intensity. Seek out thick and syrupy Australian Stickies, the local name for dessert wines that are similar to fortified Rutherglen Muscats. An aged Tawny Port would bring out the dessert's caramel and nutty notes. Don't throw away your old or stale bread—this is a great way to use it up.

1 (1 pound) loaf day-old challah or brioche, cut into ½-inch cubes

1 cup whole milk

1 cup heavy (whipping) cream

3 bananas, mashed

5 large eggs

½ cup sugar

2 teaspoons pure vanilla extract

1 teaspoon ground cinnamon

½ teaspoon sea salt

Butter, for greasing

1. Put the bread in a large bowl and set aside. In another large bowl, whisk together the milk, cream, bananas, eggs, sugar, vanilla, cinnamon, and salt until combined. Pour the milk mixture over the bread and stir to combine. Let soak in the refrigerator for 30 minutes to 1 hour.

2. Preheat the oven to 350°F.

3. Grease a 9-by-13-inch baking dish. Transfer the soaked bread and any leftover liquid to the baking dish, spreading it out evenly. Bake until golden brown and set, 50 minutes to 1 hour. Serve warm. Store leftovers in the refrigerator for up to 3 days.

Almond Biscotti

PAIR WITH:
Sweet Wines, Sparkling Wines

MAKES 20 COOKIES / PREP TIME: 20 MINUTES / BAKE TIME: 50 MINUTES

Stick to tradition when it comes to pairing wine with these dry Italian cookies. A dunk in Vin Santo is how it's done, and with good reason. The wine softens the biscotti, and you get a mouthful of sweet boozy crumbs, and an almond or two if you're lucky. Other sweet wines made from dried grapes can be just as delicious, like a Passito di Pantelleria or French Vin de Paille. For sipping, not dipping, try Moscato d'Asti or Prosecco. To create your own variations on the cookie, play with the mix-ins. You can experiment with different dried fruits, chocolate chunks, and nuts.

1½ cups slivered almonds

2½ cups all-purpose flour

1¼ teaspoons baking powder

½ teaspoon sea salt

11 tablespoons (1 stick plus 3 tablespoons) unsalted butter, at room temperature

1¼ cups sugar

2 large eggs

2 teaspoons orange zest

½ tablespoon vanilla extract

½ tablespoon almond extract

1. Preheat oven to 325°F. Line a baking sheet with parchment paper.

2. Spread the almonds on the baking sheet and toast until light golden brown, stirring occasionally, about 10 minutes. Let cool.

3. In a medium bowl, stir together the flour, baking powder, and salt.

4. In the large bowl of a stand mixer fitted with the paddle attachment, cream the butter and sugar on medium speed until fluffy, about 2 minutes. Scrape down the sides of the bowl with a spatula and, on low speed, add the eggs one at a time, beating well after each addition. Beat in the orange zest, and vanilla and almond extract. Stir in the dry ingredients and almonds until well incorporated.

5. Line a baking sheet with parchment paper. Divide the dough into 2 pieces and place them on the baking sheet. With damp hands, form the pieces into logs about 2 inches wide and 1 inch high.

6. Bake until golden brown and firm, about 30 minutes. Remove from oven and cool for about 20 minutes. Transfer to a cutting board. Using a serrated knife, cut on a bias into ½-inch slices. Put the biscotti back on the baking sheet and bake until light gold all over, turning the cookies over halfway through, about 10 minutes. Cool completely on the baking sheet. Store in an airtight container at room temperature for up to 1 month.

Cinnamon Sugar Churros

PAIR WITH:
Sweet & Fortified Wines

SERVES 4 / PREP TIME: 30 MINUTES / **COOK TIME:** 30 MINUTES

Churros—an eggy pastry piped into hot oil, deep-fried, and rolled in cinnamon sugar—are popular in Spain and Portugal, parts of Latin American, and elsewhere in the world, where they're often served for breakfast with a steaming cup of coffee or hot chocolate. This version incorporates espresso powder into the batter, a tasty homage to that morning ritual. If there was ever a perfect dessert to match the decadence of Pedro Ximénez Xérès, the sweetest, darkest style of Sherry, this is it. Coffee and sweet spices pair perfectly with this dark, concentrated wine.

1 cup water

6 tablespoons unsalted butter

5 tablespoons sugar, divided

2 teaspoons instant espresso powder

½ teaspoon vanilla extract

Pinch sea salt

1 cup all-purpose flour

1 large egg

1½ teaspoons ground cinnamon

Canola oil, for frying

1. In a large saucepan, stir the water, butter, 1 tablespoon of sugar, the espresso powder, vanilla, and salt over medium heat and bring to a boil.

2. Reduce the heat to low and add the flour all at once, stirring constantly, until the dough pulls away from the edges of the saucepan, about 4 minutes. Remove from the heat and cool for 15 minutes.

3. Stir in the eggs one at a time, beating well with a wooden spoon after each addition.

4. Transfer the churro mixture to a large cloth pastry bag fitted with a large (number 8) star piping tip.

5. In a medium bowl, stir together the remaining 4 tablespoons of sugar and the cinnamon. Set aside.

6. In a large heavy-bottomed saucepan, heat 3 inches of oil to 350°F. (A pinch of flour will sizzle when added to the oil.) Working carefully, squeeze 3-inch-long strips of batter into the hot oil, using a knife or scissors to cut the dough off at the tip. Squeeze about 4 strips per batch and fry, turning once, until golden brown, about 4 minutes. Remove with a slotted spoon, drain on a paper towel–lined plate, and repeat with the remaining batter.

7. Toss the warm churros in the cinnamon sugar and serve.

Chocolate Truffle Semifreddo with Toasted Hazelnuts

PAIR WITH:
Sweet & Fortified Wines, Sparkling Wines

SERVES 8 / PREP TIME: 20 MINUTES, PLUS CHILLING AND FREEZING TIME /
COOK TIME: 20 MINUTES

A semifreddo is a lazy man's ice-cream cake—a creamy, semi-frozen Italian dessert that can be sliced and served right out of the freezer. Chocolate and hazelnut, a classic Italian flavor combination—think gianduja and Nutella—makes it a good match for Brachetto d'Acqui, a red sparkling wine from Piedmont, a region known for its hazelnuts. A vintage Port is also a great match for chocolate. When preparing the semifreddo, don't skimp on whipping the egg whites and yolks, as volume is essential for creating the light texture.

1 cup hazelnuts	1 cup whole milk	⅔ cup sugar
2 tablespoons cocoa powder	1 teaspoon vanilla extract	¼ cup water
4 large eggs, separated	¼ teaspoon sea salt	
1 cup heavy (whipping) cream	6 ounces 70 percent dark chocolate, chopped	

1. Preheat the oven to 350°F.

2. Spread the hazelnuts on a baking sheet and toast until the skins loosen and the nuts take on some color, about 10 minutes. Transfer the nuts to a clean kitchen towel, fold it over, and rub the nuts through the towel to remove the skins. Chop the nuts and set aside.

3. In a medium bowl, whisk the cocoa to get rid of any lumps. Whisk in the yolks until smooth, then set aside.

4. In a large saucepan, heat the cream, milk, vanilla, and salt over medium-high heat until just simmering, about 5 minutes. Remove from the heat. Slowly drizzle half of the hot milk mixture into the egg mixture, whisking constantly, then slowly whisk the egg mixture into the hot milk mixture. Cook the custard on medium heat, whisking, until it's thick and smooth and coats the back of a spoon, about 5 minutes.

5. Remove from the heat, add the chocolate, and whisk until very smooth. Strain the mixture through a fine-mesh sieve into a large bowl. Cover with plastic wrap, pressing it to the surface of the custard. Refrigerate until cool.

6. In a medium saucepan, heat the sugar and water over medium-low heat. Cook until the sugar is dissolved, stirring frequently. Increase the heat to medium, bring the syrup a boil, and cook until the temperature reaches 250°F on a candy thermometer.

7. Meanwhile, beat the egg whites in the bowl of a stand mixer fitted with the whisk attachment until soft peaks form.

8. Pour the hot syrup into the egg whites in a thin stream while beating until stiff, glossy peaks form. Set aside.

9. Using an electric mixer, beat the chocolate custard until light and fluffy. Using a spatula, fold in the egg white mixture by hand until no white streaks remain.

10. Transfer the mixture to a 9-by-5-inch loaf pan and sprinkle with the hazelnuts. Cover with plastic wrap and freeze until firm, about 3 hours.

11. Let the semifreddo sit at room temperature for 10 minutes before slicing and serving. Store in the freezer for up to 1 week.

Coffee Crème Brûlée

PAIR WITH:
● Sweet & Fortified Wines ● Aromatic Whites

SERVES 6 / PREP TIME: 20 MINUTES, PLUS CHILLING TIME / **COOK TIME:** 40 MINUTES

This is like café au lait in dessert form—a velvety, eggy custard flavored with espresso powder, topped with a hard sugar crust that must be cracked to get to the pudding-like dessert below. A winning pairing with a crème brûlée is Sauternes or other botrytised sweet wine, such as Tokaj. These unctuous wines are not as cloying as other dessert wines because of their vibrant acidity, but still pair nicely with the cream and burnt sugar. For a surprising choice, opt for Gewürztraminer or Moscato, both highly aromatic wines that will add ripe, floral flavors to the dish.

2 cups heavy (whipping) cream	2 teaspoons instant espresso powder	6 large egg yolks
⅓ cup sugar	2 teaspoons pure vanilla extract	3 tablespoons maple sugar or sugar

1. Preheat the oven to 325°F. Place 6 (6-ounce) ramekins in a roasting pan.

2. In a large saucepan, combine the cream, sugar, espresso powder, and vanilla over medium heat, stirring to dissolve the sugar. When it comes to a simmer, remove from the heat and let cool slightly, about 10 minutes.

3. In a large bowl, whisk together the egg yolks until well combined. Slowly whisk in the cream mixture until completely incorporated. Strain through a fine-mesh sieve into a pitcher, then divide the mixture among the ramekins.

4. Place the roasting pan in the oven and pour in very hot water about 1 inch deep, taking care not to get any in the ramekins.

5. Bake until the centers are set but still a little jiggly (with an internal temperature around 170°F), about 35 minutes. Carefully remove the roasting pan and set aside for 5 minutes. Remove the ramekins from the pan and put them on a rack to cool completely.

6. Wrap the crème brûlée in plastic wrap and refrigerate for at least 4 hours or overnight.

7. When you are ready to serve, sprinkle 1 to 1½ teaspoons of sugar evenly over each crème brûlée. Melt the sugar with a small torch or broil in the oven, watching very carefully so they do not burn, until the sugar is caramelized.

VARIATION TIP: Omit the espresso powder if you prefer a vanilla baked custard.

Key Lime Coconut Pie

PAIR WITH:
● Aromatic Whites

SERVES 6 / **PREP TIME:** 30 MINUTES, PLUS CHILLING TIME / **COOK TIME:** 32 MINUTES

Nothing says summer quite like Key lime pie, except maybe a Key lime pie with a coconut crust. For this super-fragrant, almost tropical dessert, try a Muscat-based wine. They have a charming and perfumed expression that pairs well with citrus and other fruit. If you choose a Moscato d'Asti, the overall feeling will be airy and light, while a fortified Muscat du Cap Corse will give a decadent, rich texture. Key limes are more floral, smaller, and seedier than Persian limes. If you can't find them at the store, substitute regular limes instead.

FOR THE FILLING

5 large egg yolks

¾ cup sugar

½ cup Key lime juice, freshly squeezed or store-bought

2 teaspoons lime zest

⅛ teaspoon sea salt

5 tablespoons unsalted butter, cut into ½-inch chunks

FOR THE CRUST AND GARNISH

1½ cups all-purpose flour

¾ cup unsweetened shredded coconut

¼ cup sugar

⅛ teaspoon sea salt

8 tablespoons (1 stick) unsalted butter

1 large egg

Whipped cream, for garnish (optional)

Lime zest, for garnish (optional)

Raspberries, for garnish (optional)

1. To make the filling: In a medium stainless-steel bowl, whisk together the yolks, sugar, lime juice, lime zest, and salt until combined.

2. Bring a medium saucepan filled with 2 inches of water to a simmer over medium-high heat. Reduce the heat to low and put the bowl with the yolk mixture on the saucepan, making sure the bottom does not touch the water. Whisk constantly, until smooth and thickened, about 7 minutes.

3. Remove the bowl from the heat and whisk in the butter until smooth. Cool to room temperature, then cover the curd with plastic wrap, pressing it down on the surface, and refrigerate for at least 2 hours.

4. To make the crust and garnish: Meanwhile, in a large bowl, mix together the flour, coconut, sugar, and salt. Add the butter and rub with your fingertips until the mixture resembles coarse crumbs. Add the egg and mix until the dough comes together when pressed. Form the dough into a disk and wrap in plastic wrap. Refrigerate for 30 minutes.

5. Preheat the oven to 350°F.

6. Take the dough out of the refrigerator and let stand for 10 minutes. Roll the dough out between two pieces of floured parchment paper into a 12-inch circle. Press the dough into a 9-inch pie plate, leaving a slight overhang. Prick all over with a fork, set a sheet of parchment paper over the crust, and fill with pie weights. Place on a baking sheet and bake for 15 minutes. Remove the parchment paper and weights and bake until golden, about 10 minutes more. Let shell cool completely.

7. Fill with lime curd, garnish with whipped cream, raspberries, and lime zest (if using), and serve. The pie can be made in advance and stored for up to 2 days in the refrigerator.

Tarte Tatin

PAIR WITH:
Sweet Wines

SERVES 8 / PREP TIME: 25 MINUTES, PLUS 30 MINUTES CHILLING TIME /
COOK TIME: 50 MINUTES

This classic French upside-down tart is a sublime expression of dark caramel, tender apples, and a buttery crust. Vidal Icewine from Ontario, with its fruity aromas and good acidity, is a perfect match. Other fine options would be sweet wines from the Loire Valley, like Coteaux du Layon or Quart de Chaume, or sweet Jurançon or Pacherenc du Vic-Bilh from Southwest France. This dessert is not meant to be perfect—a rustic look is the norm—so don't sweat an uneven crust or slightly offset apples. This is always good served with a dollop of crème fraîche.

FOR THE CRUST

1¼ cups
all-purpose flour

1 tablespoon sugar

½ teaspoon sea salt

6 tablespoons unsalted
butter, cold and cubed

1 large egg yolk

1 tablespoon freshly
squeezed lemon juice

2 to 3 tablespoons
ice water

FOR THE FILLING

6 to 8 Honeycrisp apples
(about 3¼ pounds),
peeled, cored, and
quartered

1 to 2 tablespoons
freshly squeezed
lemon juice

½ cup unsalted butter

1 cup sugar

½ teaspoon sea salt

1. To make the crust: In a large bowl, mix the flour, sugar, and salt. Add the butter and quickly blend with your fingers until the mixture resembles pea-size crumbs.

2. In a small bowl, whisk together the egg yolk and lemon juice. Add to the flour mixture and stir to combine. Add the ice water, one tablespoon at a time, mixing between additions until the dough holds together when pressed.

3. Gather the dough into a disk, cover in plastic wrap, and refrigerate for at least 30 minutes.

4. To make the filling: Put the apples in a bowl with lemon juice and stir to coat. Melt the butter in a 10-inch cast-iron or ovenproof skillet over medium heat. Add the sugar and stir to dissolve. When the mixture starts to simmer, reduce the heat to low and add the apples. Cook, covered, until tender but not soft, turning occasionally, about 15 minutes. Transfer the apples to a bowl, leaving the liquid behind. Add the salt to the skillet, increase the heat to medium-high, and simmer until the liquid is a golden caramel. Remove from the heat.

5. Preheat the oven to 425°F.

6. Remove the dough from the refrigerator and roll it into a 12-inch circle on a lightly floured surface.

7. Arrange the apple quarters over the caramel in the skillet, cut-side up, in tight concentric circles. Cover with the crust, tucking in the edges. Prick a hole in the center for the steam to vent. Bake until golden brown, about 35 minutes. Cool for 5 minutes, then place a serving plate over the skillet and carefully invert the tart onto the plate. Serve warm.

| **VARIATION TIP:** Try pears instead of apples, using the same method.

Chocolate-Cherry Flourless Torte

PAIR WITH:
Sweet & Fortified Wines

SERVES 8 / PREP TIME: 20 MINUTES / **COOK TIME:** 40 MINUTES

Chocolate and cherry is one of the sexiest flavor combinations, and here it is in a deep, dark, fudgy flourless torte. As it happens, chocolate and cherries are two of the best ingredients to pair with vintage or LBV Ports. The bitterness in the chocolate offsets the sweetness of the Port, and the full-bodied, concentrated texture of the wine matches the dense structure of the cake. A young vintage will bring intense fruit flavors to match the cherries, but an older one can add nutty, mature aromas.

12 tablespoons (1 stick plus 4 tablespoons) unsalted butter, diced, plus more for greasing

14 ounces 70 percent dark chocolate, chopped

6 large eggs

1 cup sugar, divided

½ teaspoon espresso powder

½ teaspoon vanilla extract

Pinch sea salt

1 cup fresh or frozen black cherries, pitted and halved (thawed and drained if using frozen)

1. Preheat the oven to 350°F. Grease a 9-inch springform pan.

2. Fill a small saucepan with 2 inches of water and bring to a simmer over medium-high heat. Reduce the heat to low and place a medium stainless-steel bowl over the pan. Put the butter and chocolate in the bowl and stir until the mixture is melted and smooth, about 4 minutes. Remove the bowl and set aside.

3. In a large bowl, beat the eggs, ½ cup of sugar, espresso powder, vanilla, and salt until thick and pale, about 7 minutes. Fold half of the chocolate mixture into the egg mixture until just combined. Then fold in the remaining chocolate mixture. Pour the batter into the springform pan and bake until the top looks dull and a toothpick inserted near the side comes out clean, about 40 minutes. The center will be slightly loose. Transfer to a wire rack and cool to room temperature.

4. While the torte is baking, cook the cherries and the remaining ½ cup sugar in a small saucepan over medium heat, stirring, until the fruit releases its juices and the sugar is dissolved, about 6 minutes. Bring to a boil, reduce the heat to low and simmer until the sauce is syrupy and the fruit is tender, about 10 minutes more. Let cool.

5. Remove the cake from the pan and serve with the cherry sauce. Store leftovers in the refrigerator for up to 3 days.

Pineapple Cheesecake

PAIR WITH:
Sweet & Fortified Wines

SERVES 8 / PREP TIME: 15 MINUTES / **COOK TIME:** 1 HOUR, 10 MINUTES

The richness of smooth cheesecake finds its retro flavor love match in heady pineapple. Cheese-friendly wines are the way to go with this dessert. Riesling or Vidal late-harvest wines will have just the right amount of tropical flavors to vibe with the pineapple, while matching the cake's creamy texture. To transform this into a piña colada cheesecake, top with rum-flavored whipped cream and a sprinkle of toasted coconut flakes.

FOR THE CRUST

1½ cups graham cracker crumbs

¼ cup sugar

5 tablespoons butter, at room temperature

FOR THE CHEESECAKE

2 (8-ounce) packages cream cheese, at room temperature

½ cup sugar

1 teaspoon vanilla extract

5 large eggs

1 (20-ounce) can crushed pineapple packed in juice, drained, with excess liquid squeezed out

1. To make the crust: Preheat the oven to 350°F.

2. In a medium bowl, mix the graham cracker crumbs, sugar, and butter together until well combined. Press the graham mixture into the bottom and an inch or two up the sides of a 9-inch springform pan. Bake until light golden brown, about 10 minutes. Let cool completely.

3. To make the cheesecake: Set the oven to 375°F. In a large bowl, beat the cream cheese with an electric mixer until very smooth, scraping down the sides of the bowl with a spatula. Add the sugar and vanilla and beat until very smooth, scraping down the sides of the bowl. Add the eggs one at a time, beating well after each addition. Stir in the pineapple.

4. Pour the mixture into the crust and bake until the cheesecake is firm but with a slight jiggle in the center, about 1 hour. Turn the oven off and prop the door open. Let the cheesecake cool in the oven for 1 hour.

5. Run a knife around the edge of the cheesecake, then cool completely in the refrigerator before serving.

Classic Panettone

SERVES 12 / PREP TIME: 20 MINUTES, PLUS RISING TIME / **COOK TIME:** 55 MINUTES

This sweet Italian holiday bread—packed with dried fruits and flavored with vanilla and sweet Marsala wine—is buttery, rich, and, yes, possible to make at home. The signature dome shape makes it a lovely edible centerpiece for a get-together, and leftovers are ideal for French toast or bread pudding. The classic pairing for panettone is always Prosecco. The light texture brought by the bubbles and the green almonds aromas match the fluffy, toasty qualities of the bread.

1 tablespoon active dry yeast

½ cup warm milk

4 large eggs, divided

12 tablespoons (1 stick plus 4 tablespoons) unsalted butter, melted

½ cup granulated sugar

Zest of 1 orange

Zest of 1 lemon

2 teaspoons vanilla extract

4 cups all-purpose flour

½ teaspoon sea salt

Canola oil, for greasing

1½ cups chopped dried fruit, such as raisins, cherries, and cranberries

¼ cup rum or Marsala wine

1 tablespoon water

Confectioner's sugar, for dusting

1. In a small bowl, sprinkle the yeast over the warm milk. Stir, cover, and set aside for at least 10 minutes. It should look foamy.

2. In a medium bowl, whisk together 3 eggs, the butter, sugar, orange zest, lemon zest, and vanilla until light and fluffy, about 5 minutes.

3. In a large bowl, stir the flour and salt together. Add the egg mixture and the yeast mixture and stir to combine. Turn the dough out onto a lightly floured work surface and knead until smooth and elastic, 7 to 10 minutes. Gather the dough into a ball. Grease a large bowl and transfer the dough to the bowl, turning to grease all over. Cover with plastic wrap and a clean kitchen cloth and put in a warm place to double in size, about 2 hours.

4. In a small bowl, soak the dried fruit in the rum.

5. Lightly grease a panettone mold with oil. If you do not have a mold, use an angel food pan or a tube pan.

6. Transfer the dough to a lightly floured surface and gently knead in the rum-soaked fruit for about 4 minutes with oiled hands. The dough will be sticky and soft.

7. Form the dough into a ball, tucking the sides under to create a little surface tension. Transfer to the panettone mold, or shape into a rope for the tube pan. Cover and let rise until doubled in size, about 1 hour.

8. Preheat the oven to 400°F.

9. In a small bowl, whisk together the remaining egg with the water. Brush the top of the dough with the egg wash and bake until golden brown, about 50 minutes. Cool at room temperature and serve dusted with confectioner's sugar. Store at room temperature for up to 5 days.

Crab Cakes
with Tangerine
Salsa (page 158),
PAIR WITH:
Sparkling Wine,
page 21

Chapter 6

Brunch, Lighter Main Dishes & Sides

Eggs Benedict with Avocado

PAIR WITH:
◯ Crisp & Edgy Whites ◯ Sparkling Wines

SERVES 4 / PREP TIME: 30 MINUTES / **COOK TIME:** 15 MINUTES

This riff on the brunch classic swaps out Canadian bacon in favor of silky sliced avocado. The result is lighter and creamier all at once—thanks in no small part to a velvety hollandaise. These rich flavors need a wine that can cut right through them, such as a vibrant Grüner Veltliner from Wachau. Look for the term "smaragd" on the label, which indicates a riper style, with all the acidity you need. For a more rustic Benedict, try using fried eggs instead of poached.

14 tablespoons (1 stick plus 6 tablespoons) unsalted butter, divided

3 large egg yolks

Juice from ½ small lemon

Pinch sea salt

2 teaspoons white vinegar

8 large eggs

4 English muffins

1 avocado, cut into ¼-inch slices

Chopped parsley or chives, for garnish

1. Melt 1 stick plus 4 tablespoons of the butter in a medium heavy-bottomed saucepan over low heat. Remove from the heat and let cool for 5 minutes.

2. Combine the egg yolks, lemon juice, and salt in a blender and blend on high for 20 seconds, or until slightly lighter in color. Keep the blender running and add the cooled butter in a thin stream. When it is done, the sauce will be thick and emulsified.

3. Bring a large saucepan with about 3 to 4 inches of water and the vinegar to a boil, then reduce to a gentle simmer. Crack an egg into a small bowl and gently slip into the simmering water. Repeat with 3 more eggs. Poach for about 3 minutes, until the whites are firm. Remove the eggs with a slotted spoon and drain on a paper towel–lined plate. Repeat with the remaining 4 eggs.

4. Toast the English muffins, butter each side with the remaining 2 tablespoons of butter, and divide them among 4 plates. Top each half with the avocado slices, a poached egg, and the hollandaise sauce. Garnish with parsley and serve.

Cheesy Cherry-Tomato
Bread Pudding

PAIR WITH:
● Friendly, Moderate Reds

SERVES 4 / PREP TIME: 10 MINUTES / **COOK TIME:** 41 MINUTES

If you like pizza, you'll love this homey tomato and cheese bread pudding, which is fragrant with basil and oregano—and what you should keep in mind when pairing it with wine. Try a food-friendly Italian red such as a Barbera or Sangiovese, which (surprise!) also go great with a slice. Feel free to experiment with different breads, like cornbread, rye, or sourdough, to add a new dimension to the texture and flavor to the dish.

1 tablespoon extra-virgin olive oil, plus more for greasing

4 to 5 slices Italian bread, cut into ½-inch cubes, crust removed (about 2 cups)

2 teaspoons minced garlic

2 pounds cherry tomatoes (about 2½ pints), halved

1 tablespoon light brown sugar

1 teaspoon sea salt

¼ teaspoon freshly ground black pepper

3 tablespoons chopped fresh basil

1 tablespoon chopped fresh oregano

½ cup grated Asiago cheese

1. Preheat the oven to 350°F. Lightly grease a 2-quart baking dish with oil and set aside.

2. In a large skillet, heat 1 tablespoon of oil over medium-high heat. Sauté the bread until golden and crispy on all sides, about 5 minutes. Add the garlic and sauté for 1 minute more. Add the tomatoes, sugar, salt, and pepper and sauté until the tomatoes start to break down, about 5 minutes. Remove the skillet from the heat and stir in the basil and oregano.

3. Spoon the tomato mixture into the baking dish and top evenly with the cheese. Bake until bubbly and browned, about 30 minutes. Serve warm. Leftovers will keep in the refrigerator in a sealed container for up to 2 days.

Mediterranean-Inspired Pasta Frittata

PAIR WITH:
● Friendly, Moderate Reds ● Sweet & Fortified Wines

SERVES 4 / PREP TIME: 15 MINUTES / COOK TIME: 1 HOUR

This pasta omelet, crammed with spinach, basil, and sweet roasted red peppers, is best matched to moderate reds, such as Merlot or Zinfandel, which mirror the earthy flavors of vegetables without overpowering them. Or highlight the brininess of the frittata with a glass of Fino Sherry—the savory and salty notes will enhance the flavors of the olives and feta. Frittata is a fabulous dish for using up leftover vegetables or cheeses of any kind, so feel free to improvise based on what's in your fridge.

6 large eggs

1 cup 2 percent milk

1 cup dry whole-wheat rotini

1 tablespoon extra-virgin olive oil

½ sweet onion, chopped

1 teaspoon minced garlic

1 cup chopped fresh baby spinach

½ cup chopped roasted red pepper

¼ cup sliced Kalamata olives

2 tablespoons chopped fresh basil

Pinch red pepper flakes

Sea salt

½ cup crumbled feta cheese

1. Preheat the oven to 350°F.

2. In a medium bowl, whisk together the eggs and milk and set aside.

3. Fill a medium saucepan three-quarters full with water and bring to a boil over high heat. Add the pasta and cook according to the package instructions until al dente. Drain.

4. While the pasta cooks, heat the oil in a 9-inch oven-safe skillet (preferably nonstick) over medium-high heat and sauté the onion and garlic until softened, about 4 minutes.

5. Add the spinach and red pepper and sauté until the spinach is wilted, about 3 minutes. Add the pasta, olives, basil, and red pepper flakes and stir to combine. Season with salt and pour in the egg mixture, shaking to disperse the eggs among the other ingredients. Sprinkle with the feta cheese and bake until the eggs are lightly browned, about 30 minutes. Cut into wedges and serve hot or at room temperature. The frittata can be stored in the refrigerator for up to 3 days or frozen for up to 1 month.

Pear & Orange Dutch Baby

PAIR WITH:
○ Sparkling Wines

SERVES 4 / PREP TIME: 15 MINUTES / **COOK TIME:** 24 MINUTES

A Dutch baby is a baked pancake that puffs up dramatically and then falls back, creating an almost custard-like center. It's an entertaining unicorn, in that it's easy to make and a guaranteed showstopper. This one, flavored with buttery sautéed pears, orange zest, and vanilla, will make your kitchen smell irresistible. You'll find similar aromas in nectar-like Moscato d'Asti. With low alcohol, sweetness, and orchard fruit flavor, it's the perfect breakfast wine.

1¼ cups whole milk

4 large eggs

¼ cup granulated sugar

2 tablespoons
orange zest

1 teaspoon pure
vanilla extract

¼ teaspoon sea salt

⅛ teaspoon
ground nutmeg

1 cup all-purpose flour

3 tablespoons
unsalted butter

2 pears, peeled, cored,
and thinly sliced

2 tablespoons
brown sugar

Maple syrup, for serving

1. Preheat the oven to 425°F.

2. In a large bowl, whisk together the milk, eggs, sugar, orange zest, vanilla, salt, and nutmeg to combine. Whisk in the flour until smooth. Set aside.

3. Melt the butter in a 9-inch cast-iron or ovenproof skillet. Add the pears and sauté until tender, about 4 minutes. Remove the skillet from the heat and arrange the pears to cover the bottom of the skillet. Pour in the batter and bake until puffy and golden, about 20 minutes. Serve warm with maple syrup.

Grilled Fruit Caprese Salad

PAIR WITH:
Crisp & Edgy Whites, Rosé Wines

SERVES 4 / PREP TIME: 25 MINUTES, PLUS STANDING TIME / **COOK TIME:** 4 MINUTES

When you think of grilling, the first thing that comes to mind isn't necessarily fruit, but maybe it should be. Direct heat adds a smoky flavor that edges the fruit into savory territory—one reason why it works so well with fresh mozzarella. To match the acidity of the fruit and the white balsamic dressing, choose a crisp white, such as a coastal Roussillon blend with Vermentino, an Assyrtiko, a Soave, or young Rueda. And keep Provence's rosés in mind. Their bright acidity and delicate fruit flavors are a good complement to the dish, and to a meal outdoors.

3 nectarines, cut into ½-inch slices

¼ seedless watermelon, cut into 3-inch squares (½-inch thick)

¼ cup extra-virgin olive oil, divided

1 pound fresh mozzarella cheese, cut into ¼-inch slices

¼ cup white balsamic vinegar

1 tablespoon honey

¼ teaspoon sea salt

Freshly ground black pepper

¼ cup chopped pistachios

¼ cup fresh basil leaves chiffonade

1. Preheat a grill to medium-high heat.

2. Pat the fruit slices dry with paper towels and brush both sides with 2 tablespoons of oil. Grill the fruit about 2 minutes per side, turning carefully. There should be visible grill marks. Set aside to cool to room temperature.

3. Arrange the nectarine, watermelon, and mozzarella cheese slices in circles on a serving platter, alternating the fruit pieces and cheese.

4. In a small bowl, whisk together the vinegar, honey, and salt. Season with pepper to taste. Drizzle the dressing over the salad, then drizzle with the remaining oil. Scatter the pistachios and basil over the salad and let stand for 30 minutes at room temperature before serving. Store any leftovers in the refrigerator for up to 2 days.

Creamy Coleslaw with Jicama

PAIR WITH:
● Crisp & Edgy Whites, Rich & Bold Whites

SERVES 4 / PREP TIME: 20 MINUTES, PLUS CHILLING TIME

Coleslaw tastes better the longer it sits, which is also what you want from the wine you'll drink with it. Saline, zesty Albariño is a favorite with cabbage, but the buttery texture of of an oak-aged Mâcon Chardonnay is an equally good pair, especially for the creamy yogurt dressing. If you can't find jicama at the grocery store, try Asian pear or fresh parsnip instead.

FOR THE
CREAMY DRESSING

½ cup mayonnaise	2 tablespoons honey	Sea salt
¼ cup Greek yogurt	2 teaspoons Dijon mustard	Freshly ground black pepper
Juice of 1 lime		

FOR THE COLESLAW

4 cups shredded Napa cabbage	5 radishes, shredded	1 tablespoon chopped fresh mint or cilantro
	2 carrots, shredded	
1 jicama, peeled and shredded	1 scallion, white and light green parts, julienned	

1. To make the creamy dressing: In a small bowl, stir together the mayonnaise, yogurt, lime juice, honey, and mustard. Season with salt and pepper and set aside.

2. To make the coleslaw: In a large bowl, combine the cabbage, jicama, radishes, carrots, scallion, and mint until well mixed. Add the dressing and stir to combine. Refrigerate for at least 30 minutes before serving to mellow the flavor. Store the salad in the refrigerator for up to 4 days.

Green Mango Salad with Peanut Sauce

PAIR WITH:
● Aromatic Whites, Crisp & Edgy Whites

SERVES 4 / PREP TIME: 25 MINUTES, PLUS CHILLING TIME

The hallmark of a green mango salad is the irresistible combination of tart, sweet, and savory flavors, punctuated with the crunch of fresh vegetables and unripe mango, and the smooth richness of peanut sauce. You'll want a highly aromatic, slightly sweet white wine to balance the dressing, with bright acidity to match the vegetables, like an off-dry Riesling or a Chenin Blanc. Another good option is a crisp Torrontés, which is lean and dry but has sweet aromas, and enough intensity to pair with the salad's umami qualities. To make it a meal, top with your favorite protein, such as shrimp, grilled pork, or poached chicken.

2 unripe (green) mangoes, peeled, pitted, and shredded or julienned

2 carrots, shredded

1 jicama, peeled and shredded

1 cup snow peas, strings removed and julienned

1 red bell pepper, julienned

1 scallion, white and green parts, thinly sliced

3 tablespoons peanut butter

Juice of 1 lime

2 teaspoons low-sodium soy sauce

1 teaspoon minced garlic

1 teaspoon honey

Pinch red pepper flakes

¼ cup chopped peanuts

2 tablespoons chopped fresh cilantro

1. In a large bowl, combine the mangoes, carrots, jicama, snow peas, bell pepper, and scallion until well mixed.

2. In a small bowl, stir together the peanut butter, lime juice, soy sauce, garlic, honey, and red pepper flakes until well combined.

3. Add the dressing to the salad and stir to combine. Top with the peanuts and cilantro and refrigerate for 30 minutes before serving to mellow the flavors. This salad can be stored in the refrigerator for up to 2 days.

INGREDIENT TIP: Unripe mangoes should be firm to the touch with very little give when pressed.

Summer Gazpacho with Asiago-Garlic Toast

PAIR WITH:
● Crisp & Edgy Whites ● Sparkling Wines ● Rosé Wines

SERVES 4 / **PREP TIME:** 15 MINUTES, PLUS CHILLING TIME / **COOK TIME:** 1 MINUTE

Cold wine, cold soup, can't lose. Nothing captures the flavor of the season quite like gazpacho, an iconic combination of high-summer produce. What makes gazpacho so refreshing—the acidity level—is also what makes it tricky to pair. Seek out whites and rosés with the highest acidity possible: Sauvignon Blanc, Verdejo, Grüner Veltliner, or even a young White Rioja.

1½ pounds tomatoes, roughly chopped

1 yellow bell pepper, roughly chopped

1 orange bell pepper, roughly chopped

½ English cucumber, chopped

¼ sweet onion, roughly chopped

3 tablespoons extra-virgin olive oil, divided

Juice of ½ lime

1 tablespoon chopped fresh basil

1½ teaspoons minced garlic, divided

Sea salt

Freshly ground black pepper

4 thin slices baguette

¼ cup shredded Asiago cheese

1. Combine the tomatoes, bell peppers, cucumber, onion, 2 tablespoons olive oil, the lime juice, basil, and 1 teaspoon of garlic in a food processor or blender, and pulse to create a chunky puree. Transfer the gazpacho to a bowl and refrigerate for at least 1 hour. Season with salt and pepper.

2. Preheat the oven to broil.

3. Put the bread on a baking sheet and brush with the remaining 1 tablespoon oil and ½ teaspoon garlic. Broil until lightly browned, about 30 seconds. Top with the cheese and broil again until the cheese is melted, about 30 seconds. Serve the soup topped with a cheese toast.

Creamy Carrot & Ginger Soup

PAIR WITH:
● Rich & Bold Whites ● Friendly, Moderate Reds

SERVES 4 / PREP TIME: 15 MINUTES / **COOK TIME:** 30 MINUTES

This elegant soup, a puree of sweet carrots and zippy ginger, shot through with cream, calls for a heavier white wine to match its rich texture and bright flavors, like a Viognier or Douro blend. Food-friendly reds like Barbera will work, too; they possess a lively acidity that plays well with spices like coriander. If you prefer more texture, skip the sieve and blend to the desired consistency.

1 tablespoon
extra-virgin olive oil

1 sweet onion, chopped

2 tablespoons peeled
grated fresh ginger

2 teaspoons
minced garlic

3 pounds carrots,
coarsely chopped

5 cups low-sodium
vegetable or
chicken broth

1 teaspoon ground
coriander

1 cup heavy
(whipping) cream

Sea salt

Freshly ground
black pepper

1. In a medium stockpot, heat the oil over medium-high heat. Sauté the onion, ginger, and garlic until fragrant and softened, about 3 minutes. Add the carrots and stir until softened, about 7 minutes. Add the broth and coriander (the broth should cover the carrots by about 1 inch) and bring it to a boil. Reduce the heat to low and simmer until the carrots are very tender, about 20 minutes.

2. Puree the soup until smooth with an immersion blender or in a food processor. For an extra-silky soup, pass through a fine-mesh sieve.

3. Transfer the soup to a large saucepan, add the cream, and set over medium-low heat, stirring until heated through. Season with salt and pepper. Serve.

Pull-Apart Garlic, Parmesan & Herb Bread

PAIR WITH:

● Crisp & Edgy Whites ● Sparkling Wines

SERVES 6 / **PREP TIME:** 15 MINUTES, PLUS RISING TIME / **COOK TIME:** 30 MINUTES

This glorified garlic bread is an ultimate comfort food. Yeasty, buttery, fragrant with herbs, and sharp with garlic flavor, the scent will lure you from anywhere in the house. A neutral wine such as Pinot Gris, Garganega, or Albariño are sufficiently thirst-quenching to complement the bread's salty goodness, as is a sparkling wine like Champagne. The interactive nature of the pull-apart loaf and its fetching Bundt-pan shape make it a perfect contribution to a potluck.

1¼ cup warm water

2 tablespoons extra-virgin olive oil, plus more for greasing

3¾ cups bread flour, plus more for kneading

1 tablespoon sugar

2¼ teaspoons instant dry yeast or bread machine yeast

1½ teaspoons sea salt

8 tablespoons (1 stick) butter, melted

2 tablespoons chopped fresh basil

2 tablespoons chopped fresh oregano

3 teaspoons minced garlic

¾ cup grated Parmesan cheese

1. In a medium bowl, mix the water and oil together. In a large bowl, stir together the flour, sugar, yeast, and salt until well combined. Add the wet ingredients to the dry ingredients and mix to form a rough dough.

2. Turn the dough out on a lightly floured surface and knead until elastic, about 7 minutes. Gather the dough in a ball and put in a large greased bowl, cover with plastic wrap and a clean kitchen cloth, and let rise until doubled, about 1 hour.

3. Transfer the dough to a lightly floured work surface and divide into 1-inch pieces.

4. In a small bowl, stir together the butter, basil, oregano, and garlic. Dip each piece of dough in the butter mixture, turning to coat, and arrange in an even layer in the bottom of a Bundt pan. Sprinkle one-third of the Parmesan cheese over the first layer. Add two more layers with the remaining dough and cheese.

5. Cover the pan loosely with plastic wrap and a clean kitchen cloth and let rise until doubled, about 30 minutes.

6. Preheat the oven to 350°F.

7. Bake until golden brown, with an internal temperature of 195°F to 200°F, about 30 minutes. Cool for 10 minutes, then remove from the pan. Serve warm.

Falafel with Tzatziki Sauce

PAIR WITH:

● Crisp & Edgy Whites, Rich & Bold Whites ● Delicate Reds

YIELDS 12 FALAFEL / PREP TIME: 25 MINUTES **/ COOK TIME:** 5 MINUTES

Crispy golden falafel seasoned with coriander, allspice, and cumin calls for fresh white wines. You'd be happy sipping a bright Assyrtiko between bites, which also goes well with the garlicky tzatziki dipping sauce. Or, try medium-bodied whites for a little substance, to match the crunchy-on-the-outside, fluffy-inside texture of the falafel, like a Douro white blend from Portugal. If you're in the mood for red, look for freshness and fruit aromas, like a Gamay, Mencía, or even a Carignan.

FOR THE TZATZIKI SAUCE

1 cup plain Greek yogurt

½ large English cucumber, grated, with the liquid squeezed out (See Tip)

Juice of ½ lime

1 tablespoon chopped fresh dill

1 tablespoon extra-virgin olive oil

1 teaspoon minced garlic

Sea salt

FOR THE FALAFEL

1 (15-ounce) can chickpeas, drained and rinsed

½ small sweet onion, finely chopped

3 tablespoons all-purpose flour

3 tablespoons finely chopped fresh parsley

2 teaspoons minced garlic

1½ teaspoons ground coriander

1 teaspoon ground cumin

½ teaspoon ground cardamom

½ teaspoon sea salt

⅛ teaspoon allspice

Canola oil, for frying

Pita bread, for serving (optional)

1. To make the tzatziki sauce: In a small bowl, stir together the yogurt, cucumber, lime juice, dill, oil, and garlic until well blended. Season with salt to taste.

2. To make the falafel: Put the chickpeas in a food processor and pulse a few times until they look like coarse crumbs. Add the onion, flour, parsley, garlic, coriander, cumin, cardamom, salt, and allspice and pulse to form a thick paste. Roll the mixture into 2-inch balls and flatten slightly with the palm of your hand.

3. In a large skillet, heat 1 inch of oil over medium-high heat to 350°F. (A pinch of flour will sizzle when added to the oil.)

4. Working in small batches, fry the falafel until golden brown all over, turning once, about 3 minutes.

5. Transfer the patties to a paper towel–lined plate and serve with pitas (if using) and tzatziki. Store leftover falafel in the refrigerator for up to 3 days. Store leftover tzatziki in the refrigerator for up to 5 days.

> **PREPARATION TIP:** Cucumber is bursting with moisture that must be squeezed out to avoid a watery sauce. Put the shredded cucumber in a fine-mesh sieve over a bowl and use the back of a spoon to squeeze out the juice. Save the refreshing liquid to use later in a cocktail.

Crab Cakes with Tangerine Salsa

PAIR WITH:

● Sparkling Wines ● Rich & Bold Whites

SERVES 4 / PREP TIME: 30 MINUTES, PLUS 1 HOUR CHILLING TIME /
COOK TIME: 8 MINUTES

Sparkling wine is a winner with fried foods, and crab cakes are no exception. You can pair this dish with Champagne, Crémant, Franciacorta, Sekt … take your pick. However, to match the bright citrus taste of the tangerine salsa, consider trying it with a Viognier, which has similar flavors that will complement the seafood and a rich, bold texture. If you have difficulty finding quality crabmeat, the recipe can be made using finely chopped cooked shrimp or salmon in the same quantity.

FOR THE SALSA

4 tangerines, peeled and chopped

Juice of ½ lime

½ red bell pepper, finely chopped

2 tablespoons chopped red onion

2 teaspoons chopped fresh mint

Sea salt

Freshly ground black pepper

FOR THE CRAB CAKES

1 pound cooked lump crabmeat, drained and picked over

½ red bell pepper, finely chopped

1 scallion, white and green parts, finely chopped

¼ cup crushed buttery crackers, such as Ritz

1 large egg

2 tablespoons mayonnaise

1 tablespoon Dijon mustard

1 teaspoon lemon zest

Pinch cayenne pepper

3 tablespoons all-purpose flour

2 tablespoons extra-virgin olive oil

1. To make the salsa: In a small bowl, stir together the tangerines, lime juice, bell pepper, red onion, and mint. Season with salt and pepper and set aside.

2. To make the crab cakes: In a large bowl, stir together the crabmeat, bell pepper, scallion, crackers, egg, mayonnaise, mustard, lemon zest, and cayenne pepper until well mixed and holds together when pressed. If the mixture is too loose, add more crushed crackers.

3. Form the crab mixture into 12 patties about ½ inch thick. Put on a plate, cover, and refrigerate for at least 1 hour to firm up.

4. Spread the flour on a plate and dredge the crab cakes until lightly coated. In a large skillet, heat the oil over medium heat and cook the crab cakes until they are golden brown, turning once, about 4 minutes per side. Serve with the tangerine salsa.

Classic Lobster Bisque

PAIR WITH:

● Rich & Bold Whites ● Delicate Reds; Friendly, Moderate Reds

SERVES 4 / PREP TIME: 40 MINUTES / **COOK TIME:** 1 HOUR

Lobster and butter go hand in hand. A sumptuous, heavily oaked Chardonnay that matches the body and texture of the rich bisque is an obvious choice. A more surprising option would be a light red. The fruitiness of a Blaufränkisch or Barbera offers a lively counterpoint to the intense flavor of the lobster shells. To dress up this opulent soup up even more, reserve a half cup of chopped lobster meat and use it as a garnish, along with a thyme sprig and drizzled cream.

Sea salt

1 (2-pound) live lobster

2 tablespoons butter

1 sweet onion, chopped

2 teaspoons minced garlic

2 celery stalks, chopped

1 carrot, chopped

1 teaspoon fresh chopped thyme

1 teaspoon fresh chopped tarragon

3 tablespoons tomato paste

Pinch cayenne pepper

3 tablespoons all-purpose flour

¾ cup Sherry

1 cup heavy (whipping) cream

1. Put a 4- or 5-quart stockpot two-thirds full of salted water over high heat and bring to a rolling boil. Add the lobster, headfirst, cover with lid, and bring the water back to a boil. Cook the lobster until bright red, 10 to 12 minutes. To check for doneness, pull on the antenna or one of the small walking legs. If they come off easily, the lobster is done. A cooked lobster will read 135°F to 140°F on a thermometer inserted in the underside of the tail, close to the body.

2. Remove the lobster with tongs and pierce the tail and body to drain any water back into the pot. Put the lobster on a cutting board. Twist off the claws and tail. Use the side of a heavy knife to crack the knuckles and the claws to remove the meat. Place the tail underside down and use the heel of your hand to press down and crack the shell. Remove the meat and cut it lengthwise to reveal the black intestinal vein. Remove the vein and chop the meat into ½-inch pieces. Put them in a bowl and refrigerate.

3. To make lobster broth, put the shells back in the water, along with the walking legs. Reduce the heat to low and simmer for 10 minutes. Strain the broth and reserve.

4. In a large saucepan, melt the butter over medium-high heat. Sauté the onion and garlic until softened, about 3 minutes. Add the celery, carrot, thyme, and tarragon and sauté 5 minutes more. Add the tomato paste and cayenne pepper and stir to coat the vegetables, about 3 minutes. Stir in the flour and cook for 2 minutes more. Add the Sherry and bring to a simmer. Simmer for 5 minutes. Add 2 cups of the reserved broth and bring to a boil. Reduce the heat to low and simmer until the soup thickens and reduces, about 25 minutes.

5. Stir in the reserved lobster meat. Puree the soup with an immersion blender or in a food processor until smooth. Stir in the cream and season with salt to taste. Serve.

INGREDIENT TIP: Leftover lobster broth will keep in the freezer for up to 3 months, or in the refrigerator for up to 5 days.

Tempura Shrimp

PAIR WITH:
Sparkling Wines ● Crisp & Edgy Whites, Aromatic Whites, Rosé Wines

SERVES 4 / PREP TIME: 20 MINUTES / **COOK TIME:** 25 MINUTES

What sets tempura apart from other fried foods is a batter that's lighter than air itself. (The secret ingredient? Very cold club soda.) Shatteringly crisp shrimp tempura is compulsively good with a glass of Cava or Crémant d'Alsace. This crowd-pleasing appetizer is also thoroughly enjoyable with a number of still wines, such as South African Chenin Blanc, Chablis, Sancerre, Provençal Rosé, or a chilled Muscadet with its delicate saline components. Use the batter to make vegetable tempura for your vegan friends.

1 ¼ cups flour

¼ teaspoon sea salt

1 cup cold club soda

1 large egg

Canola oil, for frying

1 pound shrimp, peeled and deveined

½ cup cornstarch

1. In a large bowl, whisk together the flour and salt. In a medium bowl, whisk together the club soda and egg until blended. Add the soda mixture to the flour mixture and whisk until smooth. Set aside.

2. In a large heavy-bottomed saucepan, heat 2 inches of oil until 375°F. (A pinch of flour will sizzle when added to the oil.)

3. Working in batches, dust the shrimp in the cornstarch and dip in the batter. Fry in the oil until golden, 2 to 3 minutes. Drain on a paper towel–lined plate. Repeat with the remaining shrimp and serve.

Broiled Oysters with Gremolata

PAIR WITH:
● Crisp & Edgy Whites

SERVES 4 / PREP TIME: 15 MINUTES / **COOK TIME:** 5 MINUTES

One of the most classic pairings with oysters is Muscadet. They're both delicate and saline—no wonder it's a match made in heaven. Chablis is another classic choice. With the addition of gremolata, an aromatic topping of chopped parsley, garlic, and lemon zest, you can choose a heady wine such as Sauvignon Blanc to get those same herbaceous notes.

1½ cups loosely packed parsley leaves	¼ cup extra-virgin olive oil	Freshly ground black pepper
2 garlic cloves	Coarse sea salt	24 oysters
Zest and juice of ½ lemon		

1. Combine the parsley, garlic, lemon zest, and lemon juice in a food processor and pulse until finely chopped. Transfer the mixture to a container and stir in the oil. Season with salt and pepper and set aside.

2. Preheat the oven to broil. Arrange a layer of salt on a baking sheet so the oysters don't tip over.

3. Clean the oysters under cool running water and discard any with open shells.

4. Put an oyster, curved-side down, on a folded kitchen towel and hold the oyster in place with another towel, shielding your hand with it. Using as little pressure as possible, insert a shucking knife (or a clean flat-head screwdriver) in the hinge, turning the blade to separate the top and bottom shells. Slide the knife along the top shell to release the muscle and discard the top shell. Slide the knife under the oyster in the bottom shell to release it and set the oyster in the half shell in the salt on the baking sheet. Repeat with the remaining oysters.

5. Spoon ½ teaspoon of gremolata onto each oyster and broil until the oysters curl slightly and the topping is bubbling, 3 to 5 minutes. Remove from the oven and add more gremolata, if desired. Serve.

Hoisin Chicken Lettuce Wraps

PAIR WITH:

Aromatic Whites, Rosé Wines ● Sparkling Wines ● Delicate Reds

SERVES 4 / PREP TIME: 20 MINUTES / **COOK TIME:** 17 MINUTES

A crisp lettuce leaf enveloping hoisin-kissed chicken, sautéed crunchy vegetables, chopped cashews, and floral cilantro is a near-perfect bite. Go with a bright and aromatic wine such as Riesling to complement the umami in the hoisin sauce and the fragrant herbs. Dry rosés or a nice fruity Lambrusco pick up the more acidic elements of the dish. If you want red wine, try lighter, fruity wines such as Pinot Noir or Grenache, to have enough acidity to match the dish and light tannins that won't overpower everything.

1 tablespoon extra-virgin olive oil

¾ pound boneless, skinless chicken breasts, cut into ½-inch chunks

2 teaspoons minced garlic

1 cup finely shredded cabbage

1 large carrot, shredded

2 scallions, white and green parts, chopped

3 tablespoons hoisin sauce

Juice of ½ lime

1 tablespoon chopped fresh cilantro

8 large Boston or butter lettuce leaves

¼ cup chopped cashews

1. In a large skillet, heat the oil over medium-high heat. Add the chicken and sauté until cooked through and lightly browned, about 6 minutes. Add the garlic and sauté for 3 minutes. Add the cabbage, carrot, and scallions and sauté until the vegetables are tender, about 6 minutes. Add the hoisin sauce and lime juice and sauté until well mixed, about 2 minutes. Remove the skillet from the heat and stir in the cilantro.

2. Spoon the filling into the lettuce leaves and top with the cashews. Leftover filling can be stored in the refrigerator for up to 2 days.

Open-Faced Smoked Salmon Sandwiches

PAIR WITH:
Crisp & Edgy Whites, Aromatic Whites

SERVES 4 / PREP TIME: 25 MINUTES

This homage to smørrebrød, the Danish open-faced sandwich, combines buttery smoked salmon, snappy apple slices, and fresh cheese spread on hearty rye bread for a light, elegant meal. Crisp, light wines with good body and texture, such as Grüner Veltliner, Riesling, Torrontés, and Chablis, are excellent choices with salmon. If you'd like to swap out the salmon for some rare roast beef or smoked turkey, try an easygoing red like a Mencía, Grenache, or Valpolicella Classico.

4 tablespoons Skyr or plain Greek yogurt

1 tablespoon freshly squeezed lemon juice

Pinch sugar

Pinch sea salt

2 tablespoons cream cheese, at room temperature

4 slices dark rye bread

½ pound thinly sliced smoked salmon

1 Honeycrisp apple, cored and very thinly sliced

6 radishes, very thinly sliced

¼ red onion, very thinly sliced (optional)

1 teaspoon coarsely chopped fresh dill

1. In a small bowl, stir together the yogurt, lemon juice, sugar, and salt until blended. Set aside.

2. Spread the cream cheese on the bread and arrange the smoked salmon on top, dividing among the sandwiches. Top with the apple, radishes, onion (if using), and a generous dollop of cream sauce. Garnish with the dill and serve.

Pork Dumplings
with Spinach & Sesame

PAIR WITH:
● Aromatic Whites ● Sparkling Wines

SERVES 4 / PREP TIME: 40 MINUTES / **COOK TIME:** 30 MINUTES

These habit-forming crisp-skinned pork dumplings, with a ginger-kissed filling packed with greens and scallions and nutty sesame oil, shine with an aromatic white wine like Gewürztraminer. The ginger and sesame bring out the wine's delicate spice. If you choose a vinegar-based dipping sauce for the dumplings, consider drinking bubbles such as Champagne or Crémant, which can handle the acidity.

1 cup fresh
baby spinach

½ cup finely shredded
Napa cabbage

1 pound ground pork

2 scallions, both white
and green parts,
finely chopped

1 tablespoon soy sauce

2 teaspoons peeled
grated fresh ginger

1 teaspoon toasted
sesame oil

36 round dumpling
wrappers or wonton
wrappers

1 large egg, beaten

3 tablespoons canola
oil, divided

1 cup water, divided

1. Place a small saucepan three-quarters full of water over high heat and bring to a boil. Add the spinach and cabbage and simmer until tender, about 4 minutes. Drain in a fine-mesh sieve, squeezing the excess water out with the back of a large spoon, and finely chop the greens.

2. In a medium bowl, mix together the ground pork, spinach, cabbage, scallions, soy sauce, ginger, and sesame oil until well mixed. Refrigerate until ready to use.

3. Put a wrapper on a clean work surface and keep the others covered with a cloth to prevent them from drying out. Spoon a generous tablespoon of filling in the center of the wrapper and spread it a little toward the edges. Moisten the edges of the wrapper with the beaten egg and gently fold over to form a half-moon. Crimp the edges to seal. Repeat with the remaining wrappers and filling.

4. In a large nonstick skillet, heat 1 tablespoon of canola oil over medium-high heat. Add one-third of the dumplings and cook until the bottoms are golden brown, about 2 minutes. Add ⅓ cup of water (it will splatter, so be careful), cover, and steam for 3 minutes. Remove the lid and cook until the bottoms are crisp and browned, and all the liquid is gone, about 3 minutes more. Transfer the dumplings to a plate, wipe out the skillet, and cook two more batches with the remaining oil, dumplings, and water. Serve with your favorite dipping sauce.

Molasses Baked Beans with Salt Pork

PAIR WITH:
● Friendly, Moderate Reds; Powerful Reds

SERVES 4 TO 6 / **PREP TIME:** 30 MINUTES, PLUS SOAKING TIME / **COOK TIME:** 4 HOURS

Baked beans are one of the great comfort foods. This saucy, slow-cooked dish mixes sweet molasses, rich salt pork, starchy navy beans, and tangy flavors like mustard, vinegar, and tomato paste. It checks all the boxes. What you'll need for this thick potage is a bold, jammy wine. Zinfandel has a touch of sweetness and rich fruitiness that will accentuate the texture. Try Australian Shiraz or Portuguese blends to get concentration and rich fruit flavors. Serve the beans on toast British-style, or with a couple of sizzling hot dogs and Creamy Coleslaw with Jicama (page 150) to make it a meal.

½ pound dried navy beans

½ teaspoon sea salt

1 sweet onion, quartered

1 carrot, cut into 2-inch chunks

1 celery stalk, cut into 2-inch pieces

3 garlic cloves

½ pound salt pork, diced

½ sweet onion, chopped

½ cup unsweetened apple juice

½ cup dark molasses

¼ cup brown sugar

¼ cup tomato paste

3 tablespoons Dijon mustard

2 tablespoons apple cider vinegar

Sea salt

1. In a medium bowl, cover the beans and salt with cold water by 2 inches and soak overnight. Drain the beans and rinse in cold water.

2. Preheat the oven to 325°F.

3. In a large Dutch oven, combine the beans, quartered onion, carrot, celery, and garlic and cover with water by 2 inches. Put over medium-high heat and bring to a boil. Cover the dish and bake until the beans are tender, about 1 hour. Remove from the oven and discard the vegetables.

4. In a large skillet over medium-high heat, sauté the pork until the fat renders out and it is lightly browned, about 5 minutes. Add the chopped onion and sauté until tender, about 3 minutes. Add the bacon mixture to the beans along with the apple juice, molasses, brown sugar, tomato paste, mustard, and vinegar.

5. Return the beans to the oven, uncovered, and bake until very tender, about 3 hours. Check the beans every 30 minutes or so, adding boiling water if needed, to keep the beans covered for the first 2 hours of the cooking time. Do not add liquid for the last hour of cooking. Stir every hour so the beans at the bottom are brought to the top. The beans should not be dry and the sauce should be thick. Leftover beans can be stored in the refrigerator for up to 4 days.

Gratin Dauphinois

PAIR WITH:
Rich & Bold Whites

SERVES 4 / PREP TIME: 25 MINUTES / **COOK TIME:** 50 MINUTES

Cream, butter, cheese, potatoes. It doesn't get much better than gratin Dauphinois, a scalloped potato dish in which thinly sliced tubers all but melt in a luxurious cloak of dairy. Rich and creamy recipes call for rich and creamy wines. Bold, intense white Rhône blends, such as a white Châteauneuf-du-Pape or white Hermitage, play the role beautifully and are especially well suited for a strong cheese like Gruyère.

2 pounds russet potatoes, peeled and cut into ⅛-inch slices

1 tablespoon butter, at room temperature

3 cups whole milk

2 cups heavy (whipping) cream

2 garlic cloves, crushed

¼ teaspoon ground nutmeg

Sea salt

Freshly ground black pepper

1 cup finely shredded Gruyère cheese, shredded on the small holes of a box grater

1. Put the sliced potatoes on a clean tea towel, cover with another clean towel, and set aside.

2. Preheat the oven to 350°F.

3. Grease a 9-by-13-inch baking dish with the butter.

4. In a medium saucepan, bring the milk, cream, garlic, and nutmeg to a boil over medium-high heat. Remove from the heat, strain into a pitcher, and set aside.

5. Layer half the potato slices in the baking dish and season with salt and pepper. Pour half the milk mixture over the potatoes and sprinkle with half the cheese. Repeat with the remaining potatoes, milk mixture, and cheese.

6. Bake until the potatoes are very tender and the sauce is thick and bubbling, 40 to 45 minutes. Serve immediately. Store in the refrigerator for up to 3 days.

PREPARATION TIP: Use a mandoline to slice the potatoes or the attachment on a food processor. This will ensure uniform slices and a dish that cooks evenly.

Lamb Sliders with Brie

PAIR WITH:

● Friendly, Moderate Reds; Powerful Reds

SERVES 4 / PREP TIME: 20 MINUTES / **COOK TIME:** 14 MINUTES

These savory lamb sliders, full of fresh herbs and topped with peppery arugula, creamy Brie, and sweet blackberry preserves, are a bit more complex than your typical beef burger. Thus, they must be paired accordingly. Lean lamb wants a lighter-bodied red wine, such as a Mourvèdre, Blaufränkisch, or a Grenache-based blend from the Rhône Valley or Languedoc-Roussillon, such as a Côtes du Rhône or Terrasses du Larzac. These wines' gamey, spicy notes will complement the unique taste of lamb as well as the pungent arugula.

2 teaspoons extra-virgin olive oil

½ sweet onion, chopped

2 teaspoons minced garlic

1 pound lean ground lamb

1 teaspoon chopped fresh mint

1 teaspoon chopped oregano

Sea salt

8 soft slider buns

4 tablespoons blackberry preserves, apricot preserves, or date jam

8-ounces Brie, cut into ¼-inch slices, at room temperature

1 cup baby arugula

1. In a medium skillet, heat the oil over medium-high heat. Sauté the onion and garlic until softened, about 4 minutes. Transfer to a medium bowl and let cool for 10 minutes.

2. Add the lamb, mint, and oregano and mix until well combined. Season with salt. Divide the mixture into 8 patties, about 2½ inches in diameter and 1 inch thick.

3. Preheat a grill to medium-high heat. Grill the burgers to the desired doneness, about 5 minutes per side for medium (with an internal temperature of 160°F). Remove from the heat and let rest for 5 minutes.

4. Split the buns, spread with the preserves and top with the burger, a slice of Brie, and some arugula and serve. Store leftover patties in the refrigerator for up to 3 days.

Beef Empanadas

PAIR WITH:
● Powerful Reds

YIELDS 12 EMPANADAS / PREP TIME: 30 MINUTES / **COOK TIME:** 53 MINUTES

These golden, flaky, spiced meat turnovers are a national dish all over South and Central America, in the Caribbean, and elsewhere—a testament to their undeniable appeal. For a classic pairing, choose a strong, tannic wine that can handle the richness of the beef and the buttery pastry such as a Tempranillo or a Portuguese red blend. Argentinian Malbec or Tannat from Uruguay are also good bets, as well being geographical buddies with the dish itself.

FOR THE DOUGH

2¼ cups all-purpose flour, plus more for rolling the dough

¾ teaspoon sea salt

8 tablepsoons (1 stick) unsalted butter, chilled and cut into ¼-inch cubes

2 large eggs, divided

⅓ cup ice water

1 teaspoon white vinegar

FOR THE FILLING

1 medium russet potato, cut into ¼-inch cubes

1 tablespoon extra-virgin olive oil

1 pound extra-lean ground beef

½ sweet onion, chopped

2 teaspoons minced garlic

1 small carrot, shredded

1 teaspoon ground cumin

½ teaspoon dried oregano

½ teaspoon ground cinnamon

½ teaspoon ground chili powder

¼ teaspoon sea salt

¼ cup low-sodium beef broth

1. To make the dough: In a large bowl, whisk together the flour and salt. Add the butter and rub with your fingertips until the mixture resembles coarse crumbs.

2. In a small bowl, mix 1 egg, the water, and vinegar. Add the egg mixture to the flour mixture and mix with a fork until it just holds together. Gather the dough and press together to form a ball. Flatten the ball slightly and wrap in plastic wrap. Refrigerate for 1 hour.

3. To make the filling: While the dough is chilling, fill a small saucepan three-quarters full of water and add the potato. Bring to a boil over medium-high heat, reduce the heat to low and simmer until the potato is tender, 2 to 3 minutes. Drain and set aside.

4. In a large skillet, heat the oil over medium-high heat and cook the beef until no longer pink, stirring to break it up, about 10 minutes. Add the onion and garlic and sauté until the onion is softened, about 4 minutes. Add the carrot, potatoes, cumin, oregano, cinnamon, chili powder, and salt and sauté until the spices are fragrant, about 1 minute. Add the broth and reduce the heat to medium-
low. Simmer until the vegetables are very tender and most of the broth is absorbed, about 5 minutes.

5. Transfer the filling to a bowl and chill in the refrigerator, stirring occasionally, until the dough is cool.

6. To assemble the empanadas: Preheat the oven to 375°F. Line a baking sheet with parchment paper.

7. In a small bowl, whisk together the remaining egg with 1 tablespoon of water. Remove the dough from the refrigerator and divide into 12 equal pieces. On a lightly floured surface, roll one piece of the dough out to a thin disk about 6-inches wide. Spoon about ¼ cup of the filling onto one half of the disk, leaving a ½-inch margin around the edge. Brush the edges with egg wash and fold the other half of the dough over the filling. Use a fork or your fingertips to crimp the edges together. Transfer to the baking sheet. Repeat with the remaining dough and filling.

8. Brush the empanadas with the egg wash, prick with a fork, and bake until golden brown, about 30 minutes. Serve warm. Unbaked empanadas can be frozen for up to 1 month.

Crunchy Chopped Vegetable Tabbouleh

PAIR WITH:
Crisp & Edgy Whites, Rosé Wines

SERVES 4 / PREP TIME: 20 MINUTES / **COOK TIME:** 10 MINUTES

The fresh and earthy ingredients in this salad make it a wonderful candidate for white wine. An herbaceous Sauvignon Blanc can pair nicely with the fresh mint and parsley, whereas a fruity rosé could match the sweetness of the red bell pepper and tomatoes. Make it ahead if you can, as the flavors are more developed on the second day.

1 cup water

½ cup bulgur

1 cup finely chopped cauliflower

½ cup finely chopped broccoli

1 red bell pepper, finely chopped

¼ red onion, finely chopped

¼ cup chopped sun-dried tomatoes

¼ cup sliced Kalamata olives

½ cup finely chopped fresh parsley

2 tablespoons chopped fresh mint

¼ cup extra-virgin olive oil

Juice and zest of 1 lemon

1 teaspoon minced garlic

Sea salt

Freshly ground black pepper

1. In a small saucepan, bring the water to a boil. Add the bulgur, reduce the heat to low, cover, and simmer until tender and the water is absorbed, about 10 minutes. Remove from the heat and let stand, covered, for 10 minutes, then fluff with a fork.

2. In a large bowl, combine the cauliflower, broccoli, bell pepper, onion, tomatoes, and olives. Add the bulgur and stir to combine. Refrigerate the mixture. Once it's cool, stir in the parsley and mint.

3. In a small bowl, whisk the oil, lemon juice, and garlic, and toss with the salad. Season with salt and pepper and serve.

Maple-Roasted Parsnips with Pumpkin Seeds

PAIR WITH:
⚬ Crisp & Edgy Whites ● Friendly, Moderate Reds

SERVES 4 / PREP TIME: 10 MINUTES / **COOK TIME:** 30 MINUTES

Parsnips have a distinctly earthy taste that gets sweeter and mellower when roasted. The addition of maple syrup and warm spices to the dish nudge further in that direction, making for an exemplary autumn side. The deep flavors and meaty texture of parsnips makes them easy to pair with richer wines. An off-dry Pinot Gris brings a hint of sweetness, whereas a bigger Amarone or Ripasso would be a gutsier but still well-balanced match. Serve as a side with Braised Lamb Shanks with Rosemary & Red Wine Sauce (page 214) or Berry-Glazed Duck Breasts (page 208).

6 parsnips, peeled and cut into 1-inch chunks

1 tablespoon extra-virgin olive oil

¼ teaspoon ground nutmeg

¼ teaspoon ground cinnamon

1/8 teaspoon ground ginger

Pinch ground cloves

¼ cup maple syrup

Sea salt

¼ cup roasted pumpkin seeds

1. Preheat the oven to 400°F. Line a baking sheet with parchment paper.

2. In a large bowl, combine the parsnips, oil, nutmeg, cinnamon, ginger, and cloves until coated.

3. Spread the vegetables on the baking sheet and roast until lightly caramelized and tender, about 30 minutes, turning the vegetables over once.

4. Transfer the parsnips to a serving bowl and toss with the maple syrup. Adjust the seasoning as needed, and serve topped with pumpkin seeds.

VARIATION TIP: Add a teaspoon of butter and use a potato masher to create a mashed parsnip side, or puree in a food processor if you prefer the texture very smooth.

Braised Lamb Shanks
with Rosemary &
Red Wine Sauce (page 214),
PAIR WITH: Moderate
to Bold Reds,
pages 79 and 89

Heartier Main Dishes

Roasted Root Vegetable Borscht

PAIR WITH:
● Delicate Reds

SERVES 4 / PREP TIME: 15 MINUTES / **COOK TIME:** 45 MINUTES

Borscht has wonderfully contrasting qualities—it's sweet yet savory, light and fresh, but also hearty. To accentuate those characteristics, choose a supple, fruity red wine such as a Pinot Noir from Burgundy or New Zealand, or a Gamay. When it's hot out, try the soup chilled.

5 large beets, peeled and quartered

2 parsnips, peeled and cut into 1-inch chunks

2 carrots, cut into 1-inch chunks

2 celery stalks, cut into 1-inch chunks

1 sweet onion, quartered

2 garlic cloves, crushed

1 tablespoon extra-virgin olive oil

6 cups low-sodium vegetable broth

Juice of 1 lemon

3 tablespoons chopped fresh dill, divided

Sea salt

Freshly ground black pepper

½ cup sour cream

1. Preheat the oven to 400°F. Line a baking sheet with parchment paper.

2. In a large bowl, combine the beets, parsnip, carrots, celery, onion, and garlic with oil until well coated. Spread the vegetables on the baking sheet and roast until tender and lightly caramelized, about 40 minutes.

3. Meanwhile, heat the broth in a large saucepan over high heat until just simmering. Remove from the heat.

4. Working in batches, puree the vegetables with cups of hot broth in a blender or food processor until very smooth. Transfer the puree to a large saucepan and repeat until the broth and vegetables are used up.

5. Bring the soup to a simmer over medium heat. Stir in the lemon juice and 2 tablespoons of dill. Season with salt and pepper. Serve hot with sour cream and the remaining 1 tablespoon of dill. Store leftovers in the refrigerator for up to 3 days.

Grilled Corn Chowder

PAIR WITH:
Rich & Bold Whites

SERVES 4 / PREP TIME: 15 MINUTES / **COOK TIME:** 55 MINUTES

This recipe is a smoky twist on creamy corn chowder, made with fire-kissed kernels and grilled poblano pepper. Find a rich, full-bodied, oaked Chardonnay to match the smoky flavors and creamy texture of the soup.

4 ears fresh sweet corn, husked, silks removed

1 poblano pepper

1 tablespoon olive oil

1 sweet onion, diced

2 teaspoons minced garlic

2 celery stalks, diced

1 large russet potato, peeled and diced

½ teaspoon ground cumin

½ teaspoon ground coriander

2 cups vegetable broth

¾ cup half-and-half, plus more as needed

Juice of ½ lime

Sea salt

Freshly ground black pepper

2 teaspoons chopped fresh cilantro

1. Heat a grill to medium heat. Grill the corn and poblano pepper, turning several times, until tender and lightly charred in places, 12 to 15 minutes. You can also broil the corn and poblano on a baking sheet, turning, for about 10 minutes.

2. Immediately seal the poblano in a plastic bag, and set aside for 10 minutes. Rub the skin off, seed, and roughly chop. Set aside. Once the cobs are cool enough to handle, slice off the kernels.

3. In a large saucepan, heat the oil over medium-high heat. Sauté the onion and garlic until softened, about 4 minutes. Add the celery, potato, cumin, and coriander; sauté 3 minutes more. Stir in the broth, 3 cups of corn, and the chopped poblano. Bring the soup to a boil, then reduce the heat to low and simmer until the vegetables are tender, about 30 minutes.

4. Puree the soup in a blender until smooth, adding the half-and-half. Pour the soup back into the saucepan. Stir in the lime juice and more more half-and-half, if desired; bring back to a simmer. Season with salt and black pepper. Serve the soup topped with the remaining grilled corn and cilantro.

Shoyu-Style Ramen

PAIR WITH:
● Crisp & Edgy Whites, Aromatic Whites ● Delicate Reds

SERVES 4 / PREP TIME: 15 MINUTES / **COOK TIME:** 16 MINUTES

Ramen is a famous post-drinking food in Japan, which makes it a fun one to pair with wine. The shoyu, a soy sauce–enriched broth, is luxuriously thick and salty. It's perfect for Pinot Grigio or an off-dry Riesling, both refreshing whites that bring some balance. For a bolder choice that highlights ramen's savory umami flavor, pair with earthy red wines that are lighter in tannins such as Gamay or Mencía. This recipe gets some extra kick and umami from doubanjiang, a spicy Szechuan bean paste.

2 tablespoon toasted sesame oil

1 tablespoon peeled grated fresh ginger

2 teaspoons minced garlic

4 cups low-sodium chicken broth

3 tablespoons low-sodium soy sauce

2 tablespoons sake

1 tablespoon doubanjiang (spicy bean paste)

1 teaspoon sugar

4 (6-ounce) packages dry ramen noodles (without seasoning)

4 hard-boiled eggs, halved

Cooked pork shoulder or tenderloin, thinly sliced or shredded, for topping (optional)

Menma (fermented bamboo shoots), for topping (optional)

Chile oil or sesame oil, for topping (optional)

Chopped scallion, for topping (optional)

Nori, for topping (optional)

1. In a medium saucepan, heat the oil over medium-high heat. Sauté the ginger and garlic until softened, about 3 minutes. Add the broth, soy sauce, sake, doubanjiang, and sugar and bring to a boil. Reduce the heat to low, cover, and simmer for about 10 minutes. Remove from the heat.

2. Bring a large saucepan filled three-quarters full with water to a boil over high heat and cook the noodles according to the package instructions. Drain the noodles and divide among 4 bowls. Pour the soup into the bowls and top with the egg halves and toppings (if using). Serve immediately.

Chilled Zucchini Noodles with Coconut-Peanut Sauce

PAIR WITH:
● Aromatic Whites

SERVES 4 / PREP TIME: 25 MINUTES / **COOK TIME:** 6 MINUTES

This refreshing, low-carb zucchini noodle salad delivers on richness and flavor, thanks to a creamy, chile-spiked peanut-coconut dressing, which is still remarkably light, due to the fact that it consists mostly of raw, crunchy vegetables. A bevy of fragrant ingredients, such as jalapeño pepper, honey, and cilantro, call for a glass of Riesling. The versatile wine's vibrant acidity can clean your palate, while its fruitiness will match the intensity of the herbs and other seasonings. Aromatic whites, such as Gewürztraminer and Torrontés, will work well here, too.

1 teaspoon sesame oil

1 teaspoon minced garlic

¼ cup peanut butter

¼ cup full-fat coconut milk

2 tablespoons low-sodium soy sauce

2 tablespoons honey

Pinch red pepper flakes

Sea salt

2 large zucchini, spiralized or julienned (about 4 cups)

2 cups finely shredded cabbage, red and green (if possible)

1 cup shredded carrot

1 red bell pepper, julienned

3 scallions, sliced thinly on a bias

1 jalapeño pepper, seeded and finely chopped

½ cup chopped fresh cilantro

¼ cup chopped peanuts

1. In a small saucepan, heat the oil over medium heat. Sauté the garlic until softened and fragrant, about 3 minutes. Stir in the peanut butter, coconut milk, soy sauce, honey, red pepper flakes, and pinch of salt and stir until heated through, about 3 minutes. Remove from the heat.

2. In a large bowl, combine the zucchini, cabbage, carrot, bell pepper, scallions, jalapeño, and cilantro until mixed. Add the sauce to the vegetables and toss to combine. Season with salt to taste. Refrigerate for 2 hours before serving to let the flavors mellow. Serve topped with peanuts.

Black Bean & Corn Chilaquiles

PAIR WITH:
Sparkling Wines ● Aromatic Whites
● Delicate Reds; Friendly, Moderate Reds

SERVES 4 / PREP TIME: 15 MINUTES / **COOK TIME:** 44 MINUTES

There are few dishes more soul-satisfying then chilaquiles, a Mexican breakfast mainstay that melds crispy tortilla chips, piquant salsa, black beans, sweet corn and peppers, and fragrant aromatics in a filling casserole. Wines such as sparkling Vouvray or Crémant will have just enough sweetness to balance any spice, and a brisk acidity to cleanse the palate. For a contrasting pairing, look for fresh and fruit-driven red wines such as Grenache or Mencía. Their fresh, fruity character brighten the dish and bring new aromas forward. To give the dish a little kick, use hot salsa in the recipe.

8 (6-inch) corn tortillas

Nonstick olive oil cooking spray

2 teaspoons extra-virgin olive oil

½ sweet onion, chopped

1 red bell pepper, diced

1 teaspoon minced garlic

1 cup salsa

1 cup low-sodium canned black beans, drained and rinsed

1 cup corn kernels

½ cup chicken broth

1 teaspoon ground cumin

1 cup crumbled queso fresco cheese

Sour cream, for topping (optional)

Sliced radishes, for topping (optional)

Diced avocado, for topping (optional)

Sliced scallions, for topping (optional)

Chopped tomato, for topping (optional)

1. Preheat the oven to 325°F. Line a baking sheet with parchment paper.

2. Arrange the tortillas on the baking sheet and spray both sides lightly with the cooking spray. Bake until crisp, turning halfway through, about 25 minutes. Remove from oven and set aside to cool. Break the tortillas into 2-inch pieces when cool enough to handle.

3. Increase the oven heat to 400°F.

4. In a large oven-safe skillet, heat the oil over medium-high heat. Sauté the onions, bell pepper, and garlic until softened, about 5 minutes. Add the salsa, black beans, corn, broth, and cumin and bring to a boil. Simmer until heated through, about 4 minutes. Add the tortillas and stir to combine. Remove from the heat and top with the cheese.

5. Put in the oven and bake until the cheese is melted and the casserole is thickened, about 10 minutes. Serve with the toppings (if using). Store in the refrigerator for up to 3 days.

SUBSTITUTION TIP: Store-bought tortilla chips can be used instead of homemade. Use about 50 chips in place of the tortillas.

Pizza Margherita

PAIR WITH:

● Friendly, Moderate Reds ● Rosé Wines, Crisp & Edgy Whites

SERVES 4 / **PREP TIME:** 30 MINUTES, PLUS RISING TIME / **COOK TIME:** 40 MINUTES

This is the vanilla ice cream of pizzas, a standard-bearer that cannot be improved upon—simplicity at its best. Pizza margherita highlights a few quality ingredients: fresh basil, milky mozzarella, fruity tomatoes, and a blistering crust. One classic pairing, a bright Sangiovese such as Chianti or Rosso di Montalcino, carries the fragrance of the herbs and the mild acidity of the cheese and sauce. Crisp whites like an Albariño or a Tuscan Vernaccia are two more lively options, as is a Sangiovese-based rosado.

FOR THE DOUGH

4½ cups bread flour, plus more for kneading

2½ teaspoons active dry yeast

2 teaspoons sugar

1 teaspoon sea salt

1¾ cups warm water

3 tablespoons extra-virgin olive oil, plus more for greasing

FOR THE TOPPING

1 tablespoon extra-virgin olive oil, plus more for greasing

½ small sweet onion, chopped

1 tablespoon minced garlic

1 (28-ounce) can whole peeled tomatoes, drained

1 tablespoon chopped fresh oregano

1 teaspoon chopped fresh thyme

Sea salt

Freshly ground black pepper

1 (8-ounce) ball fresh buffalo mozzarella cheese, drained and torn into 1-inch pieces

½ bunch fresh basil leaves, torn into pieces

1. To make the dough: In a large bowl, stir together the flour, yeast, sugar, and salt until well combined. In a small bowl, stir together the water and oil. Add the wet ingredients to the dry ingredients and stir with a wooden spoon until the dough starts to come together (it will be shaggy). Turn the dough out onto a lightly floured work surface and knead for about 5 minutes, until it comes together, dusting with flour as needed. The dough should be elastic, a little tacky, but not sticking to the work surface.

2. Form the dough into a ball and transfer to a lightly oiled bowl, turning it to coat in oil. Cover the bowl with plastic wrap and a clean kitchen cloth and set aside to rise in a warm place until doubled, about 1 hour.

3. Turn the dough onto a lightly floured surface and divide it into three equal pieces. If not using all of the dough immediately, put two pieces into freezer bags and freeze for up to 2 months. Thaw overnight in the refrigerator before using.

4. Take the remaining dough and fold it over itself a few times, kneading until it's smooth and elastic.

5. To make the pizza: While the dough is rising, heat 1 tablespoon of oil in a large skillet over medium-high heat and sauté the onion and garlic until softened, about 4 minutes. Stir in the tomatoes, breaking them up with the back of the spoon. Reduce the heat and simmer until slightly thickened, about 10 minutes. Stir in the oregano and thyme and season with salt and pepper. Transfer to a bowl and cool in the refrigerator.

6. Preheat the oven to 450°F. Set a pizza stone or baking sheet in the oven.

7. Let the dough rest for about 15 minutes, so it doesn't shrink back when you spread it out.

8. Take the stone or baking sheet out of the oven and drizzle with oil.

9. Stretch the pizza dough into a 10- to 12-inch circle. Place the dough on the hot baking sheet taking care not to touch the hot metal. Spread about 1 cup of sauce on the crust, taking it to about ½ inch from the edges.

10. Scatter the mozzarella over the pizza. Scatter half the basil on the pizza. Bake until the crust is lightly browned and the cheese is bubbling, 12 to 15 minutes.

11. Remove the pizza from the oven and top with the remaining fresh basil. Slice the pizza and serve immediately.

Beet Ravioli with Ricotta Cheese, Orange, Pistachio & Parsley

Pair with:
● Crisp & Edgy Whites ● Friendly, Moderate Reds

SERVES 4 / PREP TIME: 1 HOUR, PLUS CHILLING TIME / **COOK TIME:** 44 MINUTES

This savory beet pasta, stuffed with a creamy filling flavored with orange zest, scallions, and fresh thyme, calls for a light wine that matches its silky texture and vibrant flavors. Pinot Grigio and Garganega are bright enough to contrast the creaminess of the filling. A red wine could also work, as long as the tannins are soft and the acidity is high, like a Barbera or Carignan.

FOR THE FILLING

8 ounces ricotta cheese (1 cup), drained in a fine-mesh sieve for 30 minutes

4 ounces soft goat cheese, at room temperature

1 tablespoon chopped scallion, green part only

2 teaspoons orange zest

1 teaspoon chopped fresh thyme

Sea salt

FOR THE DOUGH

2 medium red beets

1 teaspoon extra-virgin olive oil

3 large eggs

2 cups all-purpose flour, plus more for dusting

¼ teaspoon sea salt

¼ cup semolina flour, for dusting

FOR THE RAVIOLI

Sea salt

¼ cup butter

2 tablespoons extra-virgin olive oil

¼ cup chopped raw pistachios

2 tablespoons chopped fresh parsley

1. To make the filling: In a medium bowl, stir the cheeses, scallion, orange zest, and thyme and season lightly with salt. Cover and refrigerate.

2. To make the dough: Preheat the oven to 400°F. Line a pie plate with foil, put the beets on the plate, and drizzle with olive oil. Roast until tender, about 40 minutes. Remove from oven and let cool. When cool, peel and quarter the beets.

3. Puree the beets in a food processor. Add the eggs and pulse to combine. Add the all-purpose flour and salt and pulse until a ball of dough forms.

4. On a lightly floured surface, knead the dough until smooth and elastic, about 8 minutes. Wrap in plastic wrap and let rest at room temperature for about 30 minutes. Meanwhile, take the filling out of the refrigerator and let it come to room temperature.

5. Dust a baking sheet with semolina flour. Cut the dough in half, covering the second half until you are ready to use it, and run through the widest setting on the pasta maker. Flour it a bit if it sticks. Fold the dough in half and run it through again on the same setting. Continue to pass the dough through, adjusting the settings until you reach the fifth setting.

6. Cut the dough in half crosswise and trim the halves, so they are about 3 inches wide. Spoon 1 tablespoon of filling 3 inches apart on one strip, leaving a 1½-inch margin on both ends. Brush the margins all around with a little water. Cover with the second strip and press around the filling all the way around and to the edges to seal completely, eliminating any air bubbles. Cut the ravioli into 3-inch squares. Arrange them on the baking sheet; cover with a cloth. Repeat with the second piece of dough.

7. Dust the ravioli with flour and store it in the refrigerator in an airtight container between parchment paper for up to 6 hours, or freeze on the baking sheet, transfer to a container, and freeze for up to 1 month.

8. To make the ravioli: Bring a large stockpot of salted water to a boil over high heat. Reduce to a gentle boil. Add the ravioli to the boiling water and boil until tender, 3 to 4 minutes.

9. Meanwhile, heat the butter and oil in a large skillet over medium-high heat. Transfer the ravioli to the skillet using a spider and stir gently to coat. Pour into a serving dish and top with the pistachios and parsley. Serve immediately.

Roasted Vegetable Chili with Crème Fraîche

PAIR WITH:

● Friendly, Moderate Reds; Powerful Reds

SERVES 6 / PREP TIME: 25 MINUTES / **COOK TIME:** 50 MINUTES

This reimagined chili, packed with root vegetables, zucchini, sweet peppers, and two types of beans, is a hearty celebration of vegetables and legumes. Any medium-bodied red wine with a good balance of tannins and acidity will make a versatile match. Try a Syrah or GSM blend, or even something a bit bigger, like a Tempranillo, Monastrell, or Bordeaux blend. The cool crème fraîche topping elevates each bite, but in a pinch, sour cream or Greek yogurt works, too. Or hold the dairy to make it vegan.

2 tablespoons extra-virgin olive oil, divided

1 sweet potato, cut into 1-inch chunks

2 parsnips, peeled and cut into 1-inch chunks

1 sweet onion, quartered

2 zucchini, cut into 1-inch chunks

1 red bell pepper, cut into 1-inch pieces

1 yellow bell pepper, cut into 1-inch chunks

1 tablespoon minced garlic

1 (28-ounce) can fire-roasted diced tomatoes

1 (15-ounce) can navy beans, drained and rinsed

1 (15-ounce) can lentils, drained and rinsed

3 tablespoons chili powder

1 teaspoon ground cumin

½ cup crème fraîche

1 tablespoon chopped fresh cilantro

1. Preheat the oven to 400°F. Line a baking sheet with parchment paper.

2. In a large bowl, combine 1 tablespoon of oil, the sweet potato, parsnips, and onion, then spread them on the baking sheet. In the same bowl, combine the zucchini and bell peppers with 2 teaspoons of oil, and set aside.

3. Roast the sweet potato mixture for 30 minutes, stirring occasionally. Add the zucchini mixture to the baking sheet and roast for an additional 15 minutes, until tender and lightly caramelized.

4. Meanwhile, heat the remaining 1 teaspoon of oil in a large saucepan over medium-high heat. Sauté the garlic until softened, about 3 minutes. Add the tomatoes, navy beans, lentils, chili powder, and cumin and bring to a boil. Reduce to low and simmer for 10 minutes.

5. Add the roasted vegetables to the chili, stirring to combine. Serve topped with crème fraîche and cilantro. Store in the refrigerator for up to 4 days or in the freezer for up to 2 months.

SERVING TIP: Top tortilla chips with this chili, cheese, and sour cream for vegetarian nachos.

Sweet Potatoes Stuffed with Brussels Sprouts, Cranberries & Cashews

PAIR WITH:
Sweet & Fortified Wines

SERVES 4 / PREP TIME: 20 MINUTES / **COOK TIME:** 52 MINUTES

Fluffy, baked sweet potatoes filled with caramelized Brussels sprouts, tart cranberries, and crunchy cashews are like autumn on a plate. Brussels sprouts are a complicated ingredient for pairing with wine. They contain a sulfur compound that can make a perfectly good bottle taste off. Consider fortified wines like a Sercial or Verdelho Madeira, which will neutralize the compound and enhance the sweetness and nutty flavors of the dish. Keep this recipe in mind when you're planning your next Thanksgiving menu.

4 large sweet potatoes, scrubbed and pricked all over with a fork

2 tablespoons extra-virgin olive oil, divided

Sea salt

¼ sweet onion, chopped

1¼ pounds Brussels sprouts, trimmed, halved lengthwise and thinly sliced

2 tablespoons maple syrup

½ cup dried cranberries

½ cup chopped salted, dry-roasted cashews

4 tablespoons (½ stick) butter

1. Preheat the oven to 400°F.

2. Rub the sweet potatoes with 1 tablespoon of oil and season with salt. Put them on a baking sheet and bake until tender, about 40 minutes. Remove from oven and cool for 5 minutes.

3. Heat the remaining tablespoon of oil in a large skillet set over medium heat. Add the onions and sauté until they're soft and lightly golden, about 5 minutes. Add the Brussels sprouts and sauté until they're tender and bright green, about 5 minutes. Stir in the maple syrup, cranberries, and cashews and sauté for 2 minutes more. Remove from the heat and season with salt.

4. Cut the sweet potatoes in half lengthwise and push them open. Divide the butter among the split potatoes and use a fork to lightly mash and fluff the interior. Spoon the Brussels sprouts mixture into the sweet potatoes, dividing it evenly, and serve. Store in the refrigerator for up to 2 days.

> **SUBSTITUTION TIP:** Baked russets can be used in place of the sweet potatoes.

Eggplant Paprikash

PAIR WITH:
● Friendly, Moderate Reds; Powerful Reds

SERVES 4 / **PREP TIME:** 15 MINUTES / **COOK TIME:** 45 MINUTES

Paprikash is a classic Hungarian dish flavored with paprika, a highly pigmented seasoning made from ground, dried red peppers, which is the country's national spice. Although chicken is the usual base for this dish, eggplant is an inspired substitute for its meaty texture and ability to soak up flavor. Smoked paprika, used in place of the typical sweet or hot, adds a heady component that calls for a wine with savory, spicy character. Try a bottle of Mourvèdre, Merlot, or Cabernet Franc, since they have the strength and body to match such bold spices. If you prefer, serve spooned over rice or couscous instead of noodles.

1 tablespoon extra-virgin olive oil

1 sweet onion, sliced

2 teaspoons minced garlic

1½ tablespoons smoked paprika

1 (1-pound) eggplant, cut into 1-inch cubes

1 red bell pepper, thinly sliced

1 yellow bell pepper, thinly sliced

1 (14-ounce) can fire-roasted diced tomatoes, drained

½ cup low-sodium vegetable broth

½ cup sour cream

8 ounces wide egg noodles

2 tablespoons chopped fresh parsley

1. In a large skillet, heat the oil over medium-high heat and sauté the onion and garlic until softened, about 4 minutes. Add the paprika and sauté for about 2 minutes. Add the eggplant, bell peppers, tomatoes, and broth. Bring the mixture to a boil, reduce the heat to low, cover, and simmer, stirring occasionally, until the eggplant is very tender, about 25 minutes. Stir in the sour cream.

2. While the eggplant is cooking, bring a large saucepan of salted water to a boil over high heat. Cook the noodles according to the package instructions. Drain. Serve the eggplant paprikash over the noodles and top with parsley. Store in the refrigerator for up to 3 days or in the freezer for 2 months.

Gnocchi with Shiitake-Mozzarella Sauce

PAIR WITH:

● Rich & Bold Whites ● Delicate Reds; Friendly, Moderate Reds; Powerful Reds

SERVES 4 / PREP TIME: 15 MINUTES / **COOK TIME:** 24 MINUTES

Gnocchi are an excellent canvas for flavor. In this case, they're lavished in a creamy sauces, making them a natural match for full-bodied white wines. An oaked Chardonnay from Burgundy or California or a Rhône white blend work well with these rich texture and flavors. For red wines, look for vibrant acidity and earthy flavors to match the umami in the shiitakes. Aglianico, Poulsard, Mourvèdre, and Nebbiolo are all good choices.

2 tablespoons extra-virgin olive oil, divided

1 (16-ounce) package fresh potato gnocchi

½ sweet onion, chopped

2 teaspoons minced garlic

8 ounces shiitake mushrooms, stemmed and thinly sliced

1 cup low-sodium chicken broth

½ cup heavy (whipping) cream

½ cup grated Parmesan cheese

1 cup (4 ounces) shredded fresh buffalo or regular mozzarella cheese

Sea salt

Freshly ground black pepper

1 tablespoon chopped fresh parsley

1. In a large skillet, heat 1 tablespoon of oil over medium-high heat. Add the gnocchi and sauté until it is golden brown, about 7 minutes. Transfer to a medium bowl and set aside.

2. Put the skillet back on the heat and add the remaining 1 tablespoon of oil. Sauté the onion and garlic until softened, about 4 minutes. Add the mushrooms and sauté until the mushrooms are lightly caramelized, about 7 minutes. Stir in the broth, cream, and Parmesan cheese and bring to a simmer. Stir in the mozzarella cheese and simmer until the sauce is thick, about 3 minutes. Season with salt and pepper. Stir in the gnocchi and simmer until heated through, about 3 minutes. Serve topped with parsley.

Seared Scallops with Garlic-Basil Butter

PAIR WITH:
○ Crisp & Edgy Whites, Aromatic Whites

SERVES 4 / PREP TIME: 10 MINUTES / **COOK TIME:** 5 MINUTES

The subtly sweet flavor of scallops combines beautifully with pungent garlic, licoricey basil, and tart lime juice in this crowd-pleasing dish. The caramelization on the seared scallops is delicious with a rich Loire Valley dry or off-dry Chenin Blanc. But any medium-bodied white wine with good acidity will pair nicely— think dry Jurançon or Douro white blends. For a heartier serving, plate the scallops over oil-and-garlic pasta.

1 tablespoon extra-virgin olive oil

12 large sea scallops (about 1¼ pounds), with the abductor muscles removed, and rinsed and patted dry

Sea salt

Freshly ground black pepper

4 tablespoons (½ stick) butter

1 teaspoon minced garlic

Juice of 1 lime

2 tablespoons chopped fresh basil

1. In a large skillet, heat the oil over medium-high heat. Place the scallops in a single layer in the skillet. Season with salt and pepper. Sear on both sides until light golden brown, turning once, about 2 minutes per side. Transfer scallops to a plate, tent with foil, and set aside.

2. Melt the butter in the skillet and scrape up any brown bits. Add the garlic and sauté for 1 minute. Add the lime juice and basil and stir to combine. Return the scallops to the skillet along with any juices and turn them to coat in the sauce. Serve.

Mussels with Parmesan & Herbs

PAIR WITH:
Crisp & Edgy Whites   Sweet & Fortified Wines

SERVES 4 / PREP TIME: 15 MINUTES / **COOK TIME:** 9 MINUTES

This heavily aromatic preparation of mussels, redolent of fresh herbs and Parmesan cheese, is as impressive as it is easy to prepare. The saline notes of Muscadet make it an ideal pairing for seafood as well as garlic and grassy herbs. Manzanilla Sherry is also notably good with mussels for the same reason—that saline character. The mussels will be alive when you buy them, so store them loosely wrapped in the refrigerator and use them the same day.

4 tablespoons (½ stick) butter

1 sweet onion, chopped

1 tablespoon minced garlic

½ cup low-sodium chicken broth

½ cup dry white wine

2 tablespoons chopped fresh parsley

1 tablespoon chopped fresh thyme

½ tablespoon chopped fresh basil

3 pounds mussels, cleaned and rinsed (See Tip)

½ cup grated Parmesan cheese

Freshly ground black pepper

1. In a deep stockpot, melt the butter over medium-high heat. Sauté the onion and garlic until softened, about 4 minutes.

2. Increase the heat to high and add the broth, wine, parsley, thyme, and basil and bring to a boil. Add the mussels and cover. Steam, shaking the pot occasionally until the mussels are opened, about 4 to 5 minutes.

3. Remove the mussels from the heat and discard any unopened shells. Add in the Parmesan cheese, season with pepper, and serve.

> **PREPARATION TIP:** Scrub the mussels very well and debeard them by pulling out the tough, thread-like "beard" sticking out of the shell (use the flat side of a paring knife pinched between your thumb and index finger to do this job). Do this right before cooking them because debearding will kill the mussels.

Shellfish Paella

PAIR WITH:
● Rich & Bold Whites

SERVES 4 / **PREP TIME:** 20 MINUTES / **COOK TIME:** 34 MINUTES

Saffron is a highly floral spice hand-harvested from the stigma of the crocus flower. It takes more than 5,000 to produce one ounce, which is why saffron is so precious and expensive. But you need only a few strands to create wonderfully golden color and flavor in a dish like paella. The Spanish classic is a mélange of medium-grained rice with a variety of meat and savory shellfish, all infused with a saffron-tinged broth. For such a fragrant spice, the wine needs to be rich and highly flavorful. Viognier has fruity, waxy, and savory notes that will shine with paella, and the body to match all sort of proteins. A Rhône blend with Viognier, Roussane, and Marsanne are also excellent options because of their heavier body and intense flavors.

½ cup warm water

½ teaspoon saffron threads

1½ cups low-sodium chicken broth

2 tablespoons extra-virgin olive oil

8 ounces boneless, skinless chicken breast, cut into 1-inch chunks

Sea salt

Freshly ground black pepper

½ sweet onion, chopped

2 teaspoons minced garlic

1 red bell pepper, diced

1 cup Arborio rice

½ cup canned fire-roasted diced tomatoes

2 tablespoons chopped fresh parsley

1 teaspoon smoked paprika

⅛ teaspoon red pepper flakes

12 littleneck clams, scrubbed and soaked in cool water for 30 minutes

½ pound large shrimp, peeled and deveined

Juice of 1 lemon

1. In a small saucepan, stir together the water and saffron and let stand for 20 minutes. Stir in the broth and bring to a simmer over medium-high heat. Remove from the heat and set aside.

2. In a large skillet, heat the oil over medium-high heat. Season the chicken with salt and pepper and sauté until just cooked through, about 5 minutes. Transfer to a plate and set aside.

3. Add the onion and garlic to the skillet and sauté until softened, about 4 minutes. Add the bell pepper and sauté for 3 minutes more. Add the rice and sauté for 2 minutes, until coated. Add the broth mixture, tomatoes, parsley, paprika, and red pepper flakes. Bring to a boil, reduce the heat to medium-low and cook, stirring frequently, until most of the liquid is absorbed and the rice is tender, about 15 minutes.

4. Add the chicken and stir to combine. Add the clams and shrimp, nestling them into the rice. Cover with a lid or foil and cook until the shrimp is pink and the clams open, about 8 minutes. Discard any unopened clams and sprinkle the paella with lemon juice. Serve immediately. Store leftovers in the refrigerator for up to 3 days.

Ahi Tuna Tacos with Aioli

PAIR WITH:
● Delicate Reds ● Aromatic Whites; Rosé Wines

SERVES 4 / PREP TIME: 30 MINUTES / COOK TIME: 4 MINUTES

Seared tuna, cilantro-laced slaw, and creamy, garlicky aioli combine in a fish taco that's as elegant as it is summery. You can eat this dish with red, white, or rosé wines. The tuna's dense texture makes it a good fish to pair with reds that have gentle tannins, like a Blaufränkisch, Pinot Noir, or Mencía. It could also go with aromatic whites such as Riesling and Gewürztraminer, or a fresh rosé, to enhance the tacos' fresh, crisp flavors and beachy vibe. When buying the tuna, ask your fishmonger for sushi-grade, which means that it's high enough quality to be eaten raw.

FOR THE SLAW

1 English cucumber, grated and the liquid squeezed out (See Tip on page 157)

1 large tomato, seeded and chopped

1 scallion, white and green parts, chopped

Juice of 1 lime

2 tablespoons chopped fresh cilantro

FOR THE AIOLI

2 garlic cloves

½ tablespoon Dijon mustard

1 large egg

½ cup extra-virgin olive oil

½ cup canola oil

1 tablespoon freshly squeezed lemon juice

Sea salt

FOR THE TACOS

8 (6-inch) corn tortillas

1 tablespoon canola oil

1 (1-pound) sushi-grade ahi tuna fillet, about ¾ inch thick

1 teaspoon ground cumin

Sea salt

Freshly ground black pepper

1. To make the slaw: In a medium bowl, combine the cucumber, tomato, scallion, lime juice, and cilantro until well mixed. Set aside.

2. To make the aioli: Put the garlic, mustard, and egg in a blender and blend on high until very smooth. Keep the blender running and slowly add the olive oil in a thin stream. Then add the canola oil in a thin stream, until the aioli is thick and completely emulsified. Add the lemon juice and blend until smooth. Season with salt to taste. Store in the refrigerator for up to 5 days.

3. To make the tacos: Preheat the oven to 250°F.

4. Wrap the tortillas in foil and place them in the oven to warm. Meanwhile, heat the oil a large skillet over high heat. Pat the tuna dry and season with cumin, salt, and pepper. Put tuna in the skillet and cook to desired doneness, about 2½ minutes per side for medium rare. Transfer to a cutting board and let rest for 5 minutes. Cut across the grain into ¼-inch slices.

5. Take the tortillas out of the oven and lay them on a clean work surface. Evenly divide the tuna among them and top with the slaw and a tablespoon of aioli. Store the slaw for up to 3 days in the refrigerator.

Panfried Trout with Brown Butter, Dill & Fingerling Potatoes

PAIR WITH:
Crisp & Edgy Whites

SERVES 4 / PREP TIME: 15 MINUTES / **COOK TIME:** 30 MINUTES

Firm, sweet trout fillets, panfried in brown butter with aromatic shallots and garlic, are hankering for a creamy white wine to match the rich sauce. Opt for an oaked Sauvignon Blanc like Pouilly-Fumé, or a Bordeaux blend. You can also try aged White Rioja to get nutty tertiary aromas that will complement the toasted milk solids in the brown butter.

1 pound fingerling potatoes, halved lengthwise

3 tablespoons extra-virgin olive oil, divided

½ teaspoon paprika

Sea salt

Freshly ground black pepper

4 (5-ounce) skinless trout fillets, patted dry with paper towels

4 tablespoons unsalted butter, divided

¼ cup finely chopped shallot (about 4 shallots)

1 teaspoon minced garlic

1 tablespoon chopped fresh dill

1. Preheat the oven to 400°F. Line a baking sheet with parchment paper.

2. In a large bowl, combine the potatoes with 2 tablespoons of oil and the paprika. Season with salt and pepper. Spread the potatoes on the baking sheet and roast until golden brown and tender, about 30 minutes.

3. Meanwhile, season the fish with salt and pepper. In a large skillet, heat the remaining 1 tablespoon of oil and 1 tablespoon of butter over medium-high heat. Add the fish and cook, without disturbing, until lightly browned, about 3 minutes. Flip and cook until the other side is golden and the flesh is opaque, about 3 minutes more. Transfer to a serving plate and tent with foil to keep warm.

4. In the same skillet, melt the remaining 3 tablespoons of butter over medium-high heat, swirling the skillet and scraping the bottom with a wooden spoon until the butter is no longer foamy. Continue cooking until milk solids are visible and they turn a deep golden brown, about 2 minutes. Add the shallot and garlic and cook for 2 minutes longer. Drizzle the fish with the brown butter sauce, sprinkle with dill, and serve with the roasted potatoes.

Coconut-Curry Halibut en Papillote

PAIR WITH:
Crisp & Edgy Whites; Rich & Bold Whites

SERVES 4 / PREP TIME: 20 MINUTES / **COOK TIME:** 25 MINUTES

The method of cooking "en papillote," which means steaming food in packets to keep the moisture and flavor sealed in, is an easy and elegant way to prepare fish. Such is the case with this firm-fleshed halibut, cooked with thinly sliced vegetables in a gently spiced coconut-curry sauce. Choose a wine that is lean and neutral to complement the delicate, clean sea flavors of the fish, such as a Chardonnay, Pinot Grigio, or Garganega. Just be sure to avoid an oak-aged wine that would disrupt the balance and fragrant aromas of the coconut and spice. If you wish, plate the contents of the packet over fluffy white rice to serve.

2 cups shredded butternut squash

2 cups green beans or haricots verts, cut in half

1 red bell pepper, thinly sliced

1 large carrot, shredded

2 scallions, white and green parts, chopped

4 (5-ounce) halibut fillets

1 cup full-fat coconut milk

Juice of 1 lime

1 tablespoon mild curry paste

2 teaspoons peeled, grated fresh ginger

1 teaspoon minced garlic

¼ teaspoon ground coriander

⅛ teaspoon sea salt

2 tablespoons chopped fresh basil

1. Preheat the oven to 400°F. Prepare four 12-by-12-inch pieces of foil.

2. Divide the squash, beans, bell pepper, carrot, and scallions evenly among the foil pieces, piling the vegetables in the middle. Place a piece of halibut on each vegetable pile and gather up the edges of the foil to form bowls.

3. In a small bowl, mix the coconut milk, lime juice, curry paste, ginger, garlic, coriander, and salt until well blended. Spoon the sauce over the fish packets. Seal the foil into packages, tenting them above the fish mixture, and put them on a baking sheet. Bake until the fish is just cooked through, about 20 minutes. Carefully open the packets, transfer to serving plates, and top with basil.

Grilled Sirloin with Herb & Blue Cheese Compound Butter

PAIR WITH:

● Powerful Reds ○ Sweet & Fortified Wines

SERVES 4 / PREP TIME: 15 MINUTES, PLUS FREEZING TIME / **COOK TIME:** 14 MINUTES

If you really want to gild the lily, grill a premium cut of steak and top it with a pat of compound butter. The butter will melt, creating a sauce for the steak and a few moments of bliss for you. For this powerhouse duo, bring out the biggest red you have. You can't go wrong with Cabernet Sauvignon, but think even broader—Amarone has rich, concentrated dried fruit flavors that are fantastic with both steak and blue cheese, and a Châteauneuf-du-Pape is bold enough for both. And don't forget that staple pairing with blue cheese: vintage Port.

8 tablespoons (1 stick) unsalted butter, at room temperature

¼ cup crumbled blue cheese

1 tablespoon chopped fresh parsley

1 tablespoon chopped fresh basil

1 tablespoon chopped fresh oregano

1 tablespoon chopped scallion, green part only

¼ teaspoon sea salt

4 (6-ounce) top sirloin steaks

1 tablespoon extra-virgin olive oil

Sea salt

Freshly ground black pepper

1. In a small bowl, stir the butter, blue cheese, parsley, basil, oregano, scallion, and salt until well combined.

2. Place a piece of plastic wrap on a work surface and spoon the butter in a line in the middle. Fold the plastic over the butter and twist the ends to form a firm log. Put in the freezer until firm, about 1 hour.

3. Preheat the grill to medium-high heat.

4. Lightly coat the steaks with oil and season with salt and pepper. Grill the steak for about 6 to 7 minutes per side for medium (with an internal temperature of 140°F), or to desired doneness. Let the steak rest for 10 minutes and serve topped with a ½-inch slice of compound butter.

Cornish Hens with Figs & Walnuts

PAIR WITH:
● Delicate Reds

SERVES 4 / **PREP TIME:** 25 MINUTES / **COOK TIME:** 70 MINUTES

These tender little birds, baked with a nutty, fig-sweetened stuffing until golden and dripping with juices, create a real sense of occasion at the table. This is the time to splurge on your favorite Burgundian Cru, the most elegant and refined of Pinot Noirs. The dish will play off the fruitiness, spice, and earthiness of the wine, creating a most flavorful combination. If you want more structure, a Nebbiolo will also bring intense flavor to the table.

FOR THE CORNISH HENS

1 sweet onion, cut into ½-inch slices

2 carrots, cut in half lengthwise, and into 2-inch chunks

2 parsnips peeled, cut in half lengthwise, and into 2-inch chunks

4 (1½-pound) Cornish game hens, patted dry inside and outside

2 tablespoons extra-virgin olive oil

1 teaspoon smoked paprika

Sea salt

Freshly ground black pepper

3 tablespoons butter, softened

FOR THE STUFFING

1 tablespoon butter

1 cup chopped sweet onion (1 medium onion)

2 celery stalks, chopped

1 cup chicken broth

½ cup chopped dried figs

4 cups sourdough bread crumbs or corn-bread crumbs

½ cup chopped walnuts

1 teaspoon chopped fresh thyme

¼ cup store-bought balsamic reduction

1. Preheat the oven to 425°F.

2. To make the Cornish hens: Spread the onion, carrots, and parsnips in the bottom of a baking dish large enough to hold 4 Cornish hens.

3. Rub the oil all over the hens, then rub in the paprika and season with salt and pepper. Loosen the skin of the breast by running your fingers under it. Rub the butter under the skin of each hen, and set aside.

4. To make the stuffing: In a large skillet, melt the butter over medium-high heat. Sauté the onion and celery until softened, about 4 minutes. Add the broth and figs, bring the mixture to a boil, reduce the heat and simmer until the figs are plumped, about 2 minutes. Remove from the heat and stir in the bread crumbs, walnuts, and thyme. Stir to combine and season with salt and pepper.

5. Spoon the stuffing loosely into the hens, taking care not to overstuff, and tie the legs together with kitchen twine. Set the hens over the vegetables in the baking dish and roast until they're golden brown, a thermometer inserted into the thighs reaches 165°F, and the stuffing is 170°F, about an hour. Snip off the twine, arrange on a platter, and serve drizzled with balsamic reduction. Store leftovers in the refrigerator for up to 3 days, with stuffing removed from birds.

Chicken Cacciatore

PAIR WITH:
● Friendly, Moderate Reds; Powerful Reds

SERVES 4 / PREP TIME: 20 MINUTES / **COOK TIME:** 55 MINUTES

This classic Italian stew of poultry simmered until it's fall-apart tender with mushrooms, tomatoes, herbs, onions, and wine is further enhanced with the additions of potent sun-dried tomatoes and Kalamata olives. To match those deeper flavors, opt for Brunello di Montalcino, a Sangiovese with concentrated flavors and a good structure. You can also pair this dish with an Aglianico, Merlot, or a Bordeaux blend, especially Tuscan or Bolgheri wines. Instead of using pre-pared sun-dried tomatoes, try making your own by oven-drying quartered plum tomatoes in a single layer on a baking sheet overnight in a 200°F oven.

4 (5-ounce) bone-in, skinless chicken thighs

Sea salt

Freshly ground black pepper

2 tablespoons extra-virgin olive oil

1 sweet onion, chopped

1 tablespoon minced garlic

2 celery stalks, chopped

2 red bell peppers, chopped

2 tablespoons chopped fresh basil

2 tablespoons chopped fresh parsley

½ cup dry red wine

1 (28-ounce) can fire-roasted diced tomatoes

½ cup sliced Kalamata olives

½ cup chopped sun-dried tomatoes

3 tablespoons tomato paste

¼ teaspoon red pepper flakes

Rice or pasta, for serving

1. Season the chicken with salt and black pepper.

2. In a large skillet, heat the oil over medium-high heat. Brown the chicken on all sides, about 6 minutes total. Transfer the chicken to a plate and set aside.

3. Add the onion and garlic to the skillet and sauté until softened, about 4 minutes. Stir in the celery, bell pepper, basil, and parsley, and sauté until the vegetables are softened, about 6 minutes. Stir in the wine, scraping any browned bits from the bottom of the skillet, and simmer until reduced to about 2 tablespoons, about 4 minutes.

4. Stir in the diced tomatoes, olives, sun-dried tomatoes, tomato paste, and red pepper flakes and bring to a boil. Add the reserved chicken, cover, reduce the heat to low and simmer until the sauce tastes rich and the chicken is
fall-off-the-bone tender, about 35 minutes. Serve over
rice or pasta. Store in the refrigerator for up to 3 days.

> **COOKING TIP:** If you have a slow cooker, brown the chicken thighs and combine with all the ingredients in the insert. Cook on low heat for 8 to 9 hours or high heat for 4 to 5 hours.

Berry-Glazed Duck Breasts

PAIR WITH:
● Powerful Reds

SERVES 4 / **PREP TIME:** 15 MINUTES / **COOK TIME:** 20 MINUTES

Duck breast is perhaps the most luxurious cut of meat. Just imagine a rare steak but with the fattiest, most delicious skin rendered to a crisp. Adding a blackberry glaze takes it to a whole other sweet-savory level. Duck meat alone has the flavor and structure to carry heavier-bodied, tannic red wines. For instance, a simple roast duck is usually paired with a rich Pinot Noir. But for this recipe, you'll want a jammy wine with black fruit, such as Malbec or Tannat, to match the flavor of the sauce. Scoring the duck skin to ensure the fat renders evenly is easiest to do right out of the fridge, when the breast is cold and the skin is firm.

2 (1-pound) duck breasts	½ cup low-sodium chicken broth	1 cup fresh blackberries
Sea salt	½ cup red wine	1 teaspoon chopped fresh thyme
Freshly ground black pepper	2 tablespoons honey	

1. Preheat the oven to 400°F.

2. Use a sharp knife to score the duck skin, without cutting the meat, making a crosshatch pattern. Season with salt and pepper.

3. Heat a large oven-safe skillet over medium heat. Put in the duck breasts, skin-side down, and cook until the skin is crisp, about 10 minutes. Turn over and sear for 2 minutes. Turn over again, so the breasts are skin-side down, and put the skillet in the oven. Roast for 7 to 8 minutes for medium doneness, (with an internal temperature of about 140°F). Remove from oven and transfer to a cutting board to rest for 10 minutes, skin-side up.

4. Meanwhile, stir together the broth, wine, honey, and blackberries in a medium saucepan over medium-high heat. Bring to a boil, reduce the heat to medium and simmer until the sauce is reduced by three-quarters, about 10 minutes. Crush the berries lightly with the back of a spoon.

5. Cut the duck breasts on a bias into ½-inch slices. Serve topped with the berry glaze and thyme. Store leftovers in the refrigerator for up to 2 days.

Barbecue Spareribs

PAIR WITH:
● Powerful Reds ◐ Sweet & Fortified Wines

SERVES 4 / PREP TIME: 10 MINUTES / **COOK TIME:** 2 HOURS

Barbecued ribs—a balance of marbled meat, sweet-savory sauce, and a touch of char—are one of life's great pleasures. People often reach for a cold beer with their 'cue, but a fatty cut of meat like spareribs is a natural match for tannic wines. The ribs can balance a spicy Syrah or even a powerful red, such as Cabernet Sauvignon. For an even more unusual pairing, try a vintage Port or Maury Vin Doux Naturels, the latter a Grenache-based fortified wine from the South of France. Though finishing the ribs on the grill isn't necessary to cook them through, the sugars in the sauce caramelize nicely, creating a satisfying, smoky flavor.

FOR THE SAUCE

8 ounces tomato sauce

3 tablespoons no-salt-added tomato paste

3 tablespoons molasses

2 tablespoons white balsamic vinegar

1 tablespoon Dijon mustard

1 teaspoon smoked paprika

½ teaspoon garlic powder

¼ teaspoon onion powder

Sea salt

Freshly ground black pepper

FOR THE RIBS

2 tablespoons brown sugar

1 teaspoon chili powder

1 teaspoon dry mustard

4 pounds pork spareribs, silver skin removed

1. To make the sauce: In a large saucepan, stir together the tomato sauce, tomato paste, molasses, vinegar, mustard, paprika, garlic powder, and onion powder over medium heat and bring to a simmer. Reduce the heat to low and simmer for about 5 minutes longer. Season with salt and pepper and set aside.

2. To make the ribs: Preheat the oven to 325°F.

3. In a small bowl, mix the brown sugar, chili powder, and dry mustard. Rub the mixture all over the ribs, then wrap them in aluminum foil. Put them on a baking sheet and bake until very tender, about 2 hours.

4. Preheat a grill to medium. Lightly oil the grates.

5. Remove the ribs from the foil and set them on the grill. Barbecue the ribs, brushing them generously with the sauce, until lightly charred, about 4 minutes per side. If you do not have a grill, preheat the oven to broil, place the ribs on a baking sheet and broil the ribs, turning once, for about 3 minutes per side.

6. Serve with the remaining sauce. Store in the refrigerator for up to 3 days.

Smoked Meat Sandwiches with Grilled Vegetables

PAIR WITH:
● Delicate Reds, Powerful Reds

SERVES 4 / PREP TIME: 20 MINUTES / **COOK TIME:** 15 MINUTES

Montreal-style smoked meat is Canada's answer to pastrami—a cured, deli-style beef brisket encrusted in salt and spices. The combination of the intensely flavored meat, sweet grilled veggies, and zesty arugula on crusty buns makes for a sandwich that eats like a meal. Deli meat and powerful, tannic red wines are a fun low-high match. The saltiness and smokiness of the meat enhances big wines such as peppery Syrahs, structured Languedoc-Roussillon blends, and minty Chilean Cabernet Sauvignons. Some lighter reds, such as Barbera and Mencía, can lend a nice fruitiness and freshness to the smoked meat, and complement the roasted vegetables, too.

3 tablespoons extra-virgin olive oil, divided

1 tablespoon white balsamic vinegar

½ eggplant, cut into ¼-inch-thick slices

1 red bell pepper, halved

1 yellow bell pepper, halved

1 red onion, cut into ¼-inch-thick slices

1 portobella mushroom, gills scooped out

2 zucchini, cut lengthwise into ¼-inch-thick strips

Sea salt

Freshly ground black pepper

8 ounces sliced Montreal smoked meat or pastrami

4 ciabatta buns, cut in half

1 cup fresh baby arugula

1. In a large bowl, mix 2 tablespoons of oil with the vinegar. Add the eggplant, bell peppers, onion, mushroom, and zucchini and mix to coat. Season with salt and black pepper.

2. Preheat a grill to medium-high or the oven to broil.

3. Grill the vegetables until tender and lightly charred, about 9 minutes, or spread the vegetables on a baking sheet and broil, turning once, until tender and lightly charred, about 8 minutes. Transfer to a large bowl and let cool for 10 minutes. Slice the grilled peppers, eggplant, and mushrooms into ¼-inch strips and return to the bowl with the other vegetables.

4. In a medium skillet, heat the meat through over medium heat, about 5 minutes.

5. Brush the buns with the remaining 1 tablespoon of oil and grill or broil them until lightly toasted, about 1 minute. Place the bottom buns on a clean work surface and evenly divide the meat, grilled vegetables, and arugula among them, top with a bun, and serve.

SERVING TIP: Add a thick slice of Gruyère cheese to the sandwich and melt it under the broiler.

Braised Lamb Shanks with Rosemary & Red Wine Sauce

PAIR WITH:
● Friendly, Moderate Reds; Powerful Reds

SERVES 4 / PREP TIME: 20 MINUTES / **COOK TIME:** 2 HOURS, 15 MINUTES

These two steps are integral to braising and coax out the best in proteins: The browning, which creates a foundation of flavor and seals in juices, and the slow-cooking in liquid until fall-apart tender. The transformation that braised lamb shanks undergo is exemplary, changing from a tough, exercised cut to the most luscious meat imaginable. This dish pairs beautifully with Merlot and Pomerol, whose soft, velvety texture is equal to the lamb's. The meat is also a match for full-bodied reds—such as Bordeaux blends, Languedoc-Roussillon, Portuguese blends, and Malbec—because the lamb softens the wine's tannins with its supple fat. Serve this cozy dish with mashed potatoes or a root vegetable puree to soak up the sauce.

4 lamb shanks (about 2 pounds)

Sea salt

Freshly ground black pepper

2 tablespoons extra-virgin olive oil

3 medium carrots, chopped

2 celery stalks, chopped

1 sweet onion, chopped

1 tablespoon minced garlic

3 tablespoons tomato paste

1 cup red wine

3 cups low-sodium chicken broth

5 rosemary sprigs

2 bay leaves

2 tablespoons butter

1. Preheat the oven to 350°F.

2. Season the lamb shanks with salt and pepper. In a large Dutch oven or large heavy-bottomed skillet, heat the oil over medium-high heat. Sear the lamb shanks, working in batches if necessary, until browned all over, about 4 minutes per side. Transfer to a plate and set aside.

3. Add the carrots, celery, and onion to the Dutch oven and sauté until lightly caramelized, 7 to 8 minutes. Add the garlic and sauté until softened, about 3 minutes. Add the tomato paste and stir until the vegetables are coated, about 1 minute.

4. Add the wine and scrape up any brown bits in the pot. Stir in the broth, rosemary, and bay leaves and add the lamb shanks. Bring to a boil, cover, then transfer the pot to the oven. Braise until the lamb is very tender, about 2 hours. Remove the lamb from the pot, transfer to a cutting board, and tent with foil to keep warm.

5. Discard the rosemary and bay leaves. Bring the juices in the pot to a boil over medium-high heat, reduce the heat to low and simmer until the sauce is reduced by half and thickened, about 15 minutes.

6. Stir in the butter and season with salt and pepper. Remove from the heat and return the shanks to the pot, turning to coat in the sauce, and serve. Store in the refrigerator for up to 2 days.

> **SERVING TIP:** Shred the meat off the bone and serve in a pita with chopped vegetables and tzatziki.

Pappardelle with Tomato-Braised Short Ribs

PAIR WITH:
● Friendly, Moderate Reds; Powerful Reds

SERVES 4 / PREP TIME: 15 MINUTES / **COOK TIME:** 3 HOURS

Some recipes can lure you into sampling the sauce again and again. This luscious tomato-meat sauce, destined for ribbons of pappardelle, is one of them. Short ribs, slow cooked until the meat dissolves into the most succulent morsels, are shredded and added to a silky tomato sauce. Although this fatty cut may call for as many tannins as possible, the acidity of the wine still needs to match the acidity of the tomatoes. Choose intense, earthy wines with both high acidity and good structure such as Cabernet Franc, Aglianico, or Nebbiolo. If you prefer, serve over polenta instead of pasta.

2 tablespoons extra-virgin olive oil, divided

3 pounds boneless beef short ribs

Sea salt

Freshly ground black pepper

1 sweet onion, chopped

1 tablespoon minced garlic

2 carrots, finely chopped

½ cup dry red wine

¼ cup tomato paste

1 (28-ounce) can crushed San Marzano tomatoes

½ cup low-sodium beef broth

2 teaspoons dried oregano

1 teaspoon dried thyme

1 teaspoon dried basil

8 ounces pappardelle

¼ cup fresh grated Parmigiano-Reggiano cheese

1. Preheat the oven to 325°F.

2. In a large Dutch oven, heat 1 tablespoon of oil over medium-high heat. Season the short ribs with salt and pepper, add to the pot, and brown all over, about 6 minutes per side. Transfer to a plate and set aside.

3. Remove all but 1 tablespoon of fat from the Dutch oven. Add the remaining 1 tablespoon of oil and sauté the onion and garlic until softened, about 4 minutes. Add the carrots and sauté until softened and lightly browned, about 5 minutes. Stir in the wine and scrape up any brown bits in the bottom of the pot. Simmer until the wine has reduced by half, about 5 minutes. Add the tomato paste and stir to coat, about 1 minute. Add the tomatoes, broth, oregano, thyme, and basil and stir to combine. Add the short ribs and any juices from the plate, turning to coat in the sauce.

4. Bring the sauce to a simmer, then cover and put in the oven. Braise until the meat is very tender, about 2½ hours. Remove from oven and skim off most of the fat from the sauce. Transfer the meat to a cutting board and use a fork to shred it. Return the shredded meat to the sauce and season with salt and pepper.

5. Bring a large saucepan with salted water to a boil over high heat. Cook the pappardelle according to the package instructions. Drain and serve topped with the sauce and cheese. Leftover sauce can be stored in the refrigerator for up to 3 days or in the freezer for up to 1 month.

Filet Mignon with Coffee-Chocolate Sauce

PAIR WITH:
● Powerful Reds

SERVES 4 / PREP TIME: 15 MINUTES / **COOK TIME:** 32 MINUTES

Chocolate and coffee are not just for dessert. The bittersweet duo comes together beautifully in a rich, shiny sauce destined for filet mignon. It has a similar texture to a demi-glace, clinging to the steak when spooned over. For a dish like this, it's time to bring out the Cabernet Sauvignon. It works exceptionally well with chocolate and coffee, and requires protein to bolster its big, strong flavors. Consider making this dish for Valentine's Day dinner or a date night at home.

FOR THE SAUCE

2 tablespoons butter

1 sweet onion, chopped

2 teaspoon minced garlic

4 ounces red wine

½ cup espresso

2 ounces 70 percent dark chocolate

½ teaspoon chopped fresh thyme

¼ cup heavy (whipping) cream

Sea salt

Freshly ground black pepper

FOR THE STEAK

4 (5-ounce) filet mignon steaks, fat trimmed

Sea salt

Freshly ground black pepper

1 tablespoon extra-virgin olive oil

1. To make the sauce: In a large saucepan, melt the butter over medium-high heat. Add the onions and sauté until they are caramelized, about 8 minutes. Stir in the garlic and sauté until softened, about 3 minutes. Add the wine and use a spoon to scrape any brown bits from the saucepan. Bring to a boil, reduce the heat to low, and simmer until the wine is reduced by half, about 6 minutes. Add the espresso, chocolate, and thyme, and stir until the sauce is thickened and smooth, about 3 minutes. Add the cream and simmer for another minute. Season with salt and pepper and set aside

2. To make the steak: Season the steaks with salt and pepper. In a large skillet, heat the oil over medium-high heat and sear the steaks to desired doneness, 6 minutes per side for medium. Transfer to a plate and let rest for 10 minutes. Serve with the sauce. Store in the refrigerator for up to 3 days.

Six Perfect Party Pairings

The thing with party menus is that you need to have a look at the bigger picture and imagine what will be the the overall experience of the event. These six perfect party pairings will give you a head start.

Birthday Brunch

To eat:
Eggs Benedict with Avocado
(page 144)
Banana-Cinnamon Bread Pudding
(page 123)
Pear & Orange Dutch Baby (page 148)

To drink: At brunch, you often end up with a mix of rich, sweet, and salty foods. What you want is something to clean up your palate after each bite. A sparkling wine is the obvious choice (think mimosas, without the orange juice). If your menu is on the sweet side, opt for Moscato d'Asti, Prosecco, or a sweeter-style of Champagne, such as Dry or Demi-Sec. If your menu skews salty, pop some Cava or Extra Brut Champagne. Both are high in acid, which will prime your palate for the next bite.

Game-Day Feast

To eat:
Bacon-Asiago Popcorn (page 105)
Lemony Onion Rings (page 113)
Chicken Wings with Spicy Maple
Barbecue Sauce (page 118)
Pomegranate-Glazed Turkey Meatballs
(page 120)
Barbecue Spareribs (page 210)

To drink: Game-day foods are heavy! What you want is acidity to cut through the grease. Crisp white wines will never have the body and structure to stand up to these dishes, and sparkling wines will be overpowered. Look for structured reds that have good acidity, like an Argentinian Malbec or a jammy Australian Shiraz. A Brunello di Montalcino or Chianti Classico would be nice choices, too, especially if you just decide to order pizza.

Classic Cocktail Party

To eat:
Bacon-Wrapped Dates with Goat
Cheese (page 107)
Caramelized Onion Tart with Feta
Cheese & Pine Nuts (page 111)
Fig, Camembert & Arugula Flatbreads
(page 112)
Crispy Shrimp with Romesco Sauce
(page 114)
Wild Mushroom Arancini (page 116)

To drink: White wines offer versatile options for an array of appetizers that run the gamut from earthy and aromatic to rich and assertive. You can't go wrong with an unoaked Chardonnay or a Sauvignon Blanc, a Pinot Grigio, or Chenin Blanc. An equally good but often overlooked option is rosé. The crisp character will lighten the dishes and make you eager for more.

Holiday Menu

To eat:
Gratin Dauphinois (page 170)
Pull-Apart Garlic, Parmesan & Herb
Bread (page 154)
Maple-Roasted Parsnips with Pumpkin
Seeds (page 175)
Cornish Hens with Figs & Walnuts
(page 204)
Chocolate-Cherry Flourless Torte
(page 136)

To drink: Holidays are a time to indulge, which means you'll likely have a broad range of dishes to consider when pairing. A safe bet is to stick with food-friendly red wines, like a fruity Oregon Pinot Noir, Bierzo, Barbera, or Grenache. Your main dish is most likely to be a leaner cut of meat, such as turkey, chicken, or ham, which is why you want to keep your wine light yet flavorful. When it's time for dessert, spoil your guests with a wonderful Port wine.

Summer Picnic

To eat:
Summer Gazpacho with Asiago-Garlic Toast (page 152)
Mediterranean-Inspired Pasta Frittata (page 146)
Crunchy Chopped Vegetable Tabbouleh (page 174)
Heirloom Tomato & Peach Bruschetta (page 110)

To drink: For a relaxed alfresco meal, you want a refreshing wine. Rosé may be the obvious choice, though a sparkling rosé such as Cava or Champagne is just as festive and thirst quenching. A nicely chilled white, especially crisp and light options like Chablis, Vinho Verde, dry Riesling, or Grüner Veltliner, pair well with an assortment of vegetable dishes. Don't forget to bring a corkscrew, glasses, and ice packs to keep your drinks as cold as possible.

Barbecue Party

To eat:
Grilled Sirloin with Herb & Blue Cheese Compound Butter (page 203)
Creamy Coleslaw with Jicama (page 150)
Molasses Baked Beans with Salt Pork (page 168)
Grilled Fruit Caprese Salad (page 149)
Key Lime Coconut Pie (page 132)

To drink: Tannins love meat. A barbecue is the perfect time to open your heaviest, most powerful reds. Trot out your favorite Bordeaux, a big Cabernet Sauvignon, a nice Spanish Tempranillo, a Malbec, or a Syrah. Remember to chill your wines, even if they're red. The hot weather will warm them up, so it's better to keep them slightly chilled so they reach the right temperature in your glass.

Wine and Cheese Pairing Guide

CHEESE TYPE	FRESH	GOAT CHEESE	SOFT, BLOOMY	WASHED RIND
EXAMPLE	burrata, Boursin, feta, mascarpone, mozzarella, ricotta	chèvre, Crottin de Chavignol, Morbier	Brie, Camembert, Délice de Bourgogne, Neuchâtel	Fontina, Époisses, Reblochon
PAIRING	**Aromatic Whites (page 57)** Riesling **Crisp & Edgy Whites (page 43)** Pinot Grigio	**Aromatic Whites (page 57)** Riesling **Crisp & Edgy Whites (page 43)** Albariño, Sancerre, and other Sauvignon Blanc	**Sparkling Wines (page 21)** **Crisp & Edgy Whites (page 43)** Chablis and unoaked Chardonnay, Chenin Blanc, Douro Whites, Grüner Veltliner **Rich & Bold Whites (page 62)** Oaked Chardonnay, Rhône white blends	**Aromatic Whites (page 57)** Gewürztraminer, Torrontés
REASON	The acidity in these wines makes them mouthwatering companions to these fresh, creamy cheeses. The off-dry versions of the varietals will pair well with them, too.	The rich, dense textures and vibrant acidity of goat cheese must be matched (or exceeded) by the wines that go with them. Crisp whites rise to the occasion.	Wines that have good acidity can cut through the high-fat content of a soft, rich cheese for a successful contrasting pairing. If you wish to double down on the lusciousness, choose a rich white wine to match the creaminess.	Exuberant cheese needs exuberant wines. Aromatic whites match these dynamic, nuanced cheeses.

SEMI-HARD	NUTTY HARD CHEESE	AGED HARD CHEESE	BLUE
Gouda, Manchego, Roncal	**Cheddar, Comté, Emmental, Grana Padano, Gruyère, pecorino**	**Aged cheddar, aged Gouda, aged Parmigiano-Reggiano, Asiago**	**Gorgonzola, Roquefort, Stilton**
Delicate Reds (page 74) Blaufränkisch, Gamay **Friendly, Moderate Reds (page 79)** Grenache **Powerful Reds (page 89)** Mourvèdre, Syrah, Tempranillo	**Delicate Reds (page 74)** Pinot Noir **Friendly, Moderate Reds (page 79)** Sangiovese **Rich & Bold Whites (page 62)** Chardonnay, Viognier	**Friendly, Moderate Reds (page 79)** Amarone, Merlot, Zinfandel **Powerful Reds (page 89)** Aglianico, Cabernet Sauvignon	**Sweet & Fortified Wines (page 31)** Sauternes, Barsac & alternatives (page 35), Port
The nutty flavors and waxy texture of semi-hard cheeses go well with the fruity, savory aromas of red wines, but shrink in the presence of strong tannins. Try them with these mellower reds.	Medium-bodied reds and rich whites will match the texture of young hard cheeses. The nutty and complex savory notes of the cheeses need bold flavors, and these wines have them.	The older the cheese, the stronger the flavors will be, and the stronger your wine should be, which is why big reds are the way to go.	The sweetness and body of sweet and fortified wines will soften pungent, crumbly blue cheese by coating and protecting your palate.

Take-Out Pairings

BURGERS	Cabernet Sauvignon, Shiraz
CHINESE FOOD	Gewürztraminer, off-dry Riesling
FRIED CHICKEN	Grüner Veltliner, sparkling wines
INDIAN FOOD	Gamay, Grüner Veltliner, sparkling wines
MEXICAN FOOD	Albariño, Grenache, Torrontés, Zinfandel
PIZZA	Rhône red blend, Sangiovese
SUSHI	Gewürztraminer, off-dry Riesling
THAI FOOD	Chenin Blanc, Pinot Gris, Riesling

Measurement Conversions

	US STANDARD	US STANDARD (OUNCES)	METRIC (APPROXIMATE)
VOLUME EQUIVALENTS (LIQUID)	2 tablespoons	1 fl. oz.	30 mL
	¼ cup	2 fl. oz.	60 mL
	½ cup	4 fl. oz.	120 mL
	1 cup	8 fl. oz.	240 mL
	1½ cups	12 fl. oz.	355 mL
	2 cups or 1 pint	16 fl. oz.	475 mL
	4 cups or 1 quart	32 fl. oz.	1 L
	1 gallon	128 fl. oz.	4 L
VOLUME EQUIVALENTS (DRY)	⅛ teaspoon	———	0.5 mL
	¼ teaspoon	———	1 mL
	½ teaspoon	———	2 mL
	¾ teaspoon	———	4 mL
	1 teaspoon	———	5 mL
	1 tablespoon	———	15 mL
	¼ cup	———	59 mL
	⅓ cup	———	79 mL
	½ cup	———	118 mL
	⅔ cup	———	156 mL
	¾ cup	———	177 mL
	1 cup	———	235 mL
	2 cups or 1 pint	———	475 mL
	3 cups	———	700 mL
	4 cups or 1 quart	———	1 L
	½ gallon	———	2 L
	1 gallon	———	4 L
WEIGHT EQUIVALENTS	½ ounce	———	15 g
	1 ounce	———	30 g
	2 ounces	———	60 g
	4 ounces	———	115 g
	8 ounces	———	225 g
	12 ounces	———	340 g
	16 ounces or 1 pound	———	455 g

	FAHRENHEIT (F)	CELSIUS (C) (APPROXIMATE)
OVEN TEMPERATURES	250°F	120°F
	300°F	150°C
	325°F	180°C
	375°F	190°C
	400°F	200°C
	425°F	220°C
	450°F	230°C

Glossary

acidity: This is the crisp, lively character in wine. Acidity is what activates your salivary glands and makes you want another glass.

alcohol: Alcohol is the result of fermentation. Yeast transforms the natural sugars found in grapes into alcohol. Most wines will range between 12 percent and 14 percent, but can go as high as 17 percent for table wines and 22 percent for fortified wines.

appassimento: Also called "passito," this is the Italian process of drying grapes before vinification to concentrate flavors and sweetness. It's used to make Amarone and Recioto as well as Vin Santo.

appellation: An appellation defines a regulated area for wine production. Regulations state geographical delimitation as well as grape varietals and method, depending on the region.

aromatic: This term is used to define a wine that has high intensity of aromas, such as an intense smell of flowers or fruit.

autolysis: Autolysis is the chemical reaction between the wine and the lees by which enzymes break down the dead yeast cells, which produces amino acids and releases proteins and carbohydrates into the wine. It imparts characteristics such as richness and creaminess as well as aromas of bread dough, toast, or brioche. It is a key element of the traditional method of making sparkling wine, such as Champagne.

barrel: A barrel is the container used for fermenting and aging wine, which is usually made of oak. American and French oak are the most recognized, but there's also Slovenian and Hungarian oak. Shape and sizes may vary; the most recognized is the French barrique of 225 liters.

body: The body refers to the perception of volume on the palate. You could compare it with types of milk. Skim is equivalent to light-bodied wines and heavy cream is similar to full-bodied wines.

botrytis cinerea: Also called noble rot, botrytis is a mold that causes grapes to shrivel. It makes sweet, luscious wines such as Sauternes, Tokaj, Coteaux du Layon, and German Trockenbeerenauslese.

carbonic maceration: This vinification method consists of fermenting whole-cluster berries in an oxygen-free environment. The intact berries start to ferment from the inside and makes for light-bodied, juicy wines with bubblegum character. This technique is mostly used for Beaujolais Nouveau.

Charmat: Also called "tank method" or "cuve close," this is a more affordable and quicker way to make sparkling wine than the traditional method. The second fermentation takes place in a pressurized tank to a large volume of wine, instead of individually in each bottle. Wines produced from this method are usually youthful and easy drinking.

clone: A vine clone is when you take a cutting from a selected "Mother Vine" and plant it or graft it to a rootstock. It is used to genetically maintain characteristic in vines (resistance to disease, quality, flavors, etc.)

cloudy: When wine is hazy in appearance, this either means that it was intentionally not clarified or there is sediment. Natural wines and pét-nat are often cloudy.

complanted: Complantation is the art of mixing grape varieties in a terroir. This means a single vineyard will have various grape varieties all mixed together.

cru: Cru is a French term used to designate quality levels. It can be translated to "growth," e.g., Premier Cru, Grand Cru.

disgorgement/dégorgement: This is the process of removing frozen sediments from sparkling wine made using the traditional method. Through the riddling process, a gradual rotation to tilt the bottle from the side to upside down, the sediment settles in the bottle neck, which is then frozen. The crown cap is quickly removed and the sediments are expulsed.

dosage: Dosage determine the sweetness level of sparkling wines. Liqueur de dosage, a mixture of fresh wine and sugar, is added to top off wine after disgorgement.

fermentation: This is the process by which sugar is transformed into alcohol: Yeast eats sugar, then produces alcohol and carbon dioxide.

field blend: This referes to a vineyard planted with different grape varieties commingled together, which are harvested together.

flor: Flor is the layer of yeast that forms on the top of developing Sherry wines, which protects it from oxidation, and lends unique yeasty and nutty flavors.

frizzante: Frizzante is an Italian term to describe a wine that is slightly sparkling.

fumé blanc: This is the term used to describe barrel-aged Sauvignon Blanc. It was invented by Robert Mondavi.

garrigue: Garrigue are scrublands in the South of France. It's used to describe a specific bushy, herbaceous aroma that can sometimes be found in wines made close to the Mediterranean coast.

indicazione geografica tipica (IGT): Italian wines can be separated into four categories. IGT is the second quality level after vino da tavola, followed by denominazione di origine controllata (DOC) and denominazione di origine controllata e garantita (DOCG).

lees: Lees refers to the sediment left after fermentation. There are two kinds of lees: gross lees, which are the parts left by grapes (skins, pips, stems), and the fine lees, which are the dead yeast cells. Wines can be aged "sur lie," or on the fine lees, for added richness, flavor, and aroma complexity.

maceration: Maceration is the process of leaving the wine (grape juice) and skins to ferment together. It imparts the juice with more color, tannins, and aromas.

malolactic fermentation: This is the transformation of malic acid into lactic acid that gives the wine buttery flavors and a creamy texture. This step is mandatory in red wines, and can be skipped or partially or fully completed in white wines.

minerality: Minerality is a general term to describe organic matter aromas, such as rock, steel, earth, chalk, and iodine.

New World: This refers to the wine-producing regions outside of Europe with more recent wine history. ("Old World" refers to wine-producing countries in Europe with a very old winemaking history.)

oxidation: Wine that is deliberately exposed to oxygen will have a chemical change. Oxidation, although considered a fault when taken too far, is also the key to get earthy, nutty, leathery tertiary aromas.

Prädikatswein: This German quality classification is based on the level of ripeness of the grape must at harvest. Prädikatswein are divided into five levels of ascending ripeness at harvest: Kabinett, Spätlese, Auslese, Beerenauslese, and Trockenbeerenauslese. Kabinett wines are dry and the sweetness level goes up from there, reaching its peak in the very sweet Trockenbeerenauslese wines.

raisinated: This is a term for wine made from overripe grapes that have started to shrivel and dry up. These grapes have very concentrated flavors.

saignée method: This French word for "bleeding" describes a method used to produce rosé by extracting juice during the maceration of red wine, resulting in both a concentrated red wine and a rosé.

schist/schistose: This rock-based type of soil is made of layers that can crumble easily. It retains heat well and produces big, powerful wines with rich minerality. This type of soil is notably found in the Douro valley.

sélection de grains nobles: This is an Alsatian term for sweet wines made from botrytized grapes.

spumante: Spumante is an Italian term for sparkling wine.

sweetness: Sweetness in wines is referred as "residual sugar," which are the natural sugars remaining after fermentation has stopped.

tannins: This refers to phenolic compounds found primarily in the skins and pits of grapes. They're astringent and provide structure to a wine; over time tannins die off, making wines less harsh.

terroir: Terroir is a French term that refers to the combination of specific factors, such as soil, climate, and location, which can influence the character of a wine.

varietal: This refers to wines that are labeled according to the primary grape variety used to make it.

vintage: Vintage refers to a specific year that wine was made, or a specific harvest.

yeast: Yeast transforms natural sugars of grapes into alcohol. It can be found naturally in the wild, on the grapes, or it can be manufactured and added to start fermentation.

Recipe Index by Wine

Index

Acknowledgments

Writing a book about my passion has been a surreal process, a chance and a challenge that could not have been possible without the assistance that I was so lucky to get.

I have to start by thanking my awesome beloved, Michael McDuff. Thank you for your love and support, for being the perfect tasting partner, for keeping our tiny people out of my hair so I could write, and most of all, thank you for believing in me like you do.

I also want to thank Michelle Anderson for her work as recipe developer on the amazing and inspiring recipes. Working with you on this project really brought it to the next step and made it such a cool experience. I'm delighted to have been involved on this book with you and your immense expertise. Thanks to everyone on the Callisto team who helped me so much. Special thanks to Cecily McAndrews, for your honest, kind editorial notes and keen insights.

About the Author

Joanie Métivier is a sommelier and wine expert with a background in tourism, translation, and geography. She holds a certificate of the Court of Master Sommeliers, and a certification of the Wine & Spirits Education Trust (WSET) Level 3, with Distinction. She was the first Quebecer to complete the Whisky Ambassador training program. Her wine writing appears in many respected outlets, including WineTourismMag.com, *Vertdevin Magazine*, and at JoanieMetivier.com.

CPSIA information can be obtained
at www.ICGtesting.com
Printed in the USA
JSHW011947020321
12136JS00001B/1